Information Design and Distance Learning
for International Development

Information Design and Distance Learning for International Development

Rod Shaw

A Master's Thesis

Submitted in partial fulfilment of the requirements for the award of
Master of Philosophy of Loughborough University

Research Supervisors:
Dr Margaret Ince and Dr David Twigg

Director of Research:
Mr Ian Smout

Water, Engineering and Development Centre
Loughborough University
2001

WEDC

Water, Engineering and Development Centre,
Loughborough University,
Leicestershire, LE11 3TU, UK

© WEDC, Loughborough University, 2001

A catalogue record for this book is available from the British Library.

A reference copy of this publication is also available online at:
http://www.lboro.ac.uk/wedc/publications/iddlid.htm

ISBN Paperback: 978 0 90605 592 2
ISBN Ebook: 978 1 78853 305 8
Book DOI: http://dx.doi.org/10.3362/9781788533058

Shaw, R.J. (2001)
Information Design and Distance Learning for International Development
WEDC, Loughborough University, UK.

WEDC (The Water, Engineering and Development Centre) at Loughborough University in the UK is one of the world's leading institutions concerned with education, training, research and consultancy for the planning, provision and management of physical infrastructure for development in low- and middleincome countries.

This edition is reprinted and distributed by Practical Action Publishing.
Since 1974, Practical Action Publishing has published and disseminated books and information in support of international development work throughout the world. Practical Action Publishing trades only in support of its parent charity objectives and any profits are covenanted back to Practical Action (Charity Reg. No. 247257, Group VAT Registration No. 880 9924 76).

Acknowledgements

I would like to thank my research supervisors Margaret Ince, David Twigg (and posthumously, David Mack), and my Director of Research, Ian Smout for their advice and guidance throughout this research.

I would also like to thank the following for their help and support: Ruth Allen, Lois Child, Bob Elson, Richard Franceys, Tricia Jackson, John Pickford, M. Sohail, The Dean of Engineering, NUST and all those who undertook the tests.

Not least, I would like to thank my family, especially Esther, Emily, Joseph and Kate for their constant support and encouragement.

Abstract

This thesis presents an investigation by research into information design and distance learning for international development.

The purpose of the research has been to reach an understanding of how distance learning is affected by the physical design of printed study materials. In particular, the thesis examines the use of engineering drawing systems as the basis for constructing illustrations designed to support instructional texts concerned with the technical aspects of infrastructure development.

Part I of the research comprises a review of literature on the following themes: learning and adult education; international development and distance learning; information design for self-instruction; and research into illustration, with particular reference to the visual perception of engineering drawings and the implications for their cross-cultural use.

Part II presents questions and hypotheses which emerged from the literature reviewed in Part I. Part II also presents the research methodology designed to test comprehension of engineering drawing systems. It presents the results of tests undertaken by five adult learning groups selected from pre-degree, undergraduate and postgraduate populations. Part II concludes with an analysis and discussion of the results of these tests.

Part III of the thesis presents the conclusions drawn from both the literature review and from the analysis of the research results. It was found that learning is affected by the design of study materials in a number of ways. It was also found that, in the global distance learning context, the use of isometric projection to represent the three-dimensional nature of objects and structures in two dimensions is likely to be more effective than either third-angle projection or linear perspective. Part III concludes with proposals for further study.

Table of contents

PART III

List of abbreviations

DFID   Department for International Development
LUSAD   Loughborough University School of Art and Design
NUST   National University of Science and Technology (Zimbabwe)
WEDC   Water, Engineering and Development Centre

List of boxes

List of figures

xiv

List of photographs

List of tables

PART I

Chapter 1

Introduction

1.1. About this thesis

This thesis has been prepared according to the *Regulations for Higher Degrees by Research* and *Notes for the Guidance of Research Students, Directors of Research, Supervisors and Examiners* of Loughborough University. It is the final report of the investigation by research into information design and distance learning for international development.

1.2. Purpose

The purpose of this research has been to reach an understanding of how distance learning is affected by the physical design of printed study materials.

1.3. Aims

The aims of the research were:

i.   to review published literature relating to information design and distance learning;

ii. to develop and conduct a series of tests to compare the responses of subjects to different methods of presenting information;

iii. to report and analyse the results of these tests; and

iv. to draw conclusions from the research and present proposals for further investigations.

1.4. Objectives

The objectives to support the first aim were:

- to define what is meant by 'information design' and 'distance learning' within the context of this research;

- to locate relevant sources of literature;

- to examine the literature and abstract the salient views of authors; and

- to report the findings.

The objectives to support the second aim were:

- to identify existing tests relating to aspects of information design and learning;

- to review methods of testing learner responses to aspects of information design;

- to develop hypotheses relating to appropriate methods of presenting information for distance learning;

- to discuss and confirm with the research supervisors methodologies for validating the research;

- to devise tests as appropriate;

- to identify sample groups of postgraduate learners;

- to conduct pilot tests using the sample groups;

- to revise the methods of testing as appropriate; and

- to conduct revised tests.

The objectives to support the third aim were:

- to review appropriate methods of data analysis;

- to analyse, interpret and report the findings; and

- to discuss the implications of the findings.

The objectives to support the fourth aim were:

- to critically examine the literature review and research hypotheses, design, methodologies and results; and

- to identify areas for further study.

1.5. Structure of the thesis

The thesis is comprised of three parts:

Part I: **Review of Literature**

Part II: **Research Hypotheses, Design, Methodology, Results and Analysis**

Part III: Conclusions

1.5.1 Part I

Part I presents the review of literature under the following chapter headings:

Chapter 2. Learning and Adult Education

Chapter 2 introduces some of the key issues relating to learning and adult education today, providing a background for the central themes of the research discussed in subsequent chapters.

The chapter begins with the simple question: 'What is learning?' It then presents an overview of the theories and principles of learning, and examines the significance of individual differences and learning styles. It also examines the characteristics of adult learners and the optimum conditions for adult learning. It concludes with a profile of the adult learning group which is the particular focus of the research reported and discussed in Part II.

Chapter 3. International Development and Distance Learning

Chapter 3 examines the ways in which self-directed modes of learning, and in particular distance learning, can support the education and training needs of the professional adult as described in Chapter 2. It focuses on the needs of professionals whose work is involved with development in low- and middle-income countries.

The chapter begins with a discussion of the goal of international development and the need for education and training to realize this goal. It describes conventional teaching methods, and goes on to outline the distance learning alternative and the benefits and problems of this approach. It also examines ways of delivering distance learning programmes, focusing in particular on print-based materials. The chapter concludes with an examination of some of the ways in which distance learning is being used in low- and middle-income countries, especially in engineering, and for infrastructure development.

Chapter 4. Information Design for Self-Instruction

Chapter 4 defines what is meant by design for self-instruction and presents a review of the literature. This review is mainly derived from literature concerning the design of paper-based learning materials, although other research is considered where appropriate. All of the literature considered here relates to printed English.

Chapter 5. Research into Illustration

Chapter 5 continues the review of literature into information design with a discussion of research into illustration which is the focus of the study reported in Part II.

The chapter begins by describing the role of illustrations in educational materials and the factors which affect their comprehension. It goes on to examine Evelyn Goldsmith's analytical model which leads into a discussion of particular aspects of illustration. It concludes with a discussion of the visual perception of engineering drawings and the implications of their cross-cultural use.

1.5.2 Part II

Part II presents questions and hypotheses which emerged from the literature review; the research design; methodology; results; analysis; and discussion under the following chapter headings:

Chapter 6. Hypotheses

This chapter raises questions about the use of engineering drawing projection systems for illustrations designed to support distance learning in a cross-cultural context. It presents the research hypotheses and a list of variables which relate to the hypotheses. It also describes the projection systems under study.

Chapter 7. Research Methodology

This chapter describes the ways in which the hypotheses presented in Chapter 6 have been tested. Specifically, it presents: the basis of the test design; the principal requirements in experimental technique that were identified to ensure validity of the tests; the pilot test designs and methods (along with a description of the group of subjects who performed the pilot tests); discussions and conclusions relating to each test design; and the revised tests and methods (with descriptions of the groups of subjects who performed the revised tests).

Chapter 8. Results

Data compiled from the Subject Profile Forms (Appendix 1) were entered into the statistical analysis and data management system SPSS, along with the scores for the pilot tests and the revised tests. Chapter 8 presents a summary of the results of the revised tests in tabular and chart form.

Chapter 9. Data Analysis and Discussion

Chapter 9 presents a comparative analysis of the tests themselves, followed by analyses of the results for selected variables and categories. The results are analysed in this way as a means of either supporting or rejecting the hypotheses presented in Chapter 6. The extent to which analysis of the data can support or reject the hypotheses is discussed within each section.

1.5.3 Part III

Part III of the thesis (Chapter 10) presents the conclusions drawn from Parts I and II. It also identifies areas for further study.

Chapter 2

Learning and Adult Education

2.1. Introduction

The question of how people learn was the concern of many applied psychologists during the twentieth century. From theories of learning came theories of education which now affect students at all stages of life, from infancy to old age.

This chapter introduces some of the key issues of learning and adult education today, and thereby provides a background for the central themes of the research discussed in subsequent chapters.

The chapter begins with the simple question: 'What is learning?' It then presents an overview of the theories and principles of learning, and examines the significance of individual differences and learning styles. It also examines the characteristics of adult learners as well as the optimum conditions for adult learning. It concludes with a profile of the adult learning group which is the particular focus of the research reported and discussed in Part II.

2.2. What is learning?

It is apparent from the literature concerned with the nature of learning that there is very little agreement about what learning actually is. Hergenhahn (1988) cites the *American Heritage Dictionary* which defines learning as follows: 'To gain knowledge, comprehension or mastery through experience or study'. *The Concise Oxford Dictionary of Current English* (1976) defines learning simply as 'knowledge acquired by study'. Hergenhahn observes that most psychologists find such definitions unacceptable because of the nebulous terms they contain, such as knowledge, comprehension, and mastery. Smith (1983) notes that psychologists and educators do not agree on, or even claim to be able to say with great precision what learning is, only to describe its effects and how people go about it. After years of trying to synthesize learning theory, Kidd (1973: p.23) goes as far as to suggest that 'there is no answer to the question "What is learning?", any more than there is to the question "What is electricity?" '

According to Hergenhahn, the trend in recent years is to accept a definition of learning that refers to changes in observable behaviour. The most popular has been the one suggested by Kimble (1961: p.6) which defines learning 'as a relatively permanent change in behavioural potentiality that occurs as a result of reinforced practice'. Hergenhahn notes, however, that this popular definition is not accepted universally.

There is, nevertheless, general agreement that learning has to do with very complex processes that involve the whole self (Smith, 1983). According to Smith, it is possible that learning defies precise definition because it is used to describe either a product, a process or a function. When learning is used to describe a *product*, the emphasis is on the outcome of the experience. When it is used to describe a *process*, an attempt is made to account for what happens when a learning experience takes place. When learning is used to describe a *function*, the emphasis is on aspects (such as motivation) which are believed to help 'produce' learning.

2.3. Theories of learning

2.3.1 Lunzer's classification

Lunzer (1968) suggests a two-way classification of approaches to the study of learning and adaptation which is presented in Table 2.1.

Firstly, there is the widely accepted classification of theories ranging from *behaviourist* to *cognitive*, the main difference being that behaviourist psychologists see learning as a matter of links between stimulus and response, whereas cognitive theorists place greater emphasis on the functioning of the brain, internal mental thinking and the role of experience which modifies present behaviour.

Secondly, there is the classification which concerns the *role of stimuli* as the initiator of behaviour. The *reactive* view is that without stimuli there would be no response, because responses only occur when an organism needs to react to a stimulus. The active (or structural) approach sees the organism as spontaneously activated i.e. 'if there were no stimuli in the environment, the organism would seek stimuli' (Child, 1981: p.84).

In both classifications, there are those who take intermediate positions. The table, therefore, has a nine-cell structure. As Lunzer himself points out, however, this belies the considerable overlap and numerous shades of position.

Table 2.1. Cross-categorization of learning theorists

Role of the stimulus	Behaviourist	Intermediate	Cognitivist
Reactive	Watson Thorndike Hull		(Locke)
Intermediate	Pavlov	Tolman	Gestalt psychologists
Structural (or active)	Skinner	Lorenz Broadbent Lunzer	Piaget (Lewin)

Source: Child, 1981: p.84 (modified from Lunzer, 1968: p.120)

The scope of this chapter does not allow for detailed discussion of the intermediate positions, but an outline of behaviourist and cognitive theories is helpful in setting the scene for the review of the *principles* of learning which follows.

2.3.2 Behaviourist theories

J. B. Watson (1878-1958) was the earliest and most extreme behaviourist. His fundamental conclusion from many experimental observations of animal and childhood learning was that stimulus-response (S-R) connections are more likely to be established the more frequently or recently an S-R 'bond' occurs. Solving a problem might require many unsuccessful attempts before the correct solution is reached. Of the many responses made in an effort to solve a problem, the unsuccessful ones will tend not to be repeated. Trying alternative paths in the solution of problems of any kind has become known as 'trial and error' learning.

E. L. Thorndike (1874-1949) also thought that people 'stamp in' effective S-R connections and 'stamp out' those responses which are useless. Thorndike stressed the importance of satisfying and gratifying outcomes from a response so that S-R connections are reinforced whenever satisfying results are apparent. The statement that satisfaction serves to strengthen the S-R bonds is known as Thorndike's *Law of Effect*. Knowledge of results, therefore, is essential for reinforcement to take place.

Like Watson and Thorndike, I. P. Pavlov (1849-1936) viewed behaviour as responses initiated by stimuli. Pavlov's interests, however, were strictly centred on the physiological reflex actions of animals and less relevant in the study of human learning, although his studies gave rise to the process known as *classical conditioning*. Smith (1983) gives an example of a human situation which displays classical conditioning. If a child visiting a dentist for treatment which requires an injection experiences pain when he or she is first injected, the waiting area may act as a stimulus for the activation of 'autonomic reactions' such as an increase in heart beat. Where the child continues to experience pain on each visit, the conditioning is reinforced.

Similarly, positive conditioning can occur with associations of pleasurable stimuli. In particular, C. L. Hull (1884-1952) emphasized that learning takes place when human (or animal) needs are being satisfied.

Amongst behaviourists working during the second half of the last century, B. F. Skinner is perhaps the best known. His main interest was a particular type of conditioning termed *operant conditioning* as it requires the learner to 'operate on the environment': i.e. be *active*. From many animal and human experiments, Skinner drew several conclusions about learning:

- Each step of the learning process should be short and emerge from previously learned behaviour.

- In the early stages, learning should be regularly rewarded and at all stages carefully controlled by a schedule of continuous reinforcement.

- Reward should follow quickly when the correct response appears. This is commonly referred to as *feedback* and is based on the principle that motivation is enhanced when a learner is informed of his or her progress.

2.3.3 Cognitive theories

One of the main objections to the behaviourist approach to the understanding of learning is that it does not account for the diversity of human behaviour. Wertheimer, the earliest psychologist to attempt a cognitive interpretation, believed that breaking down behaviour into constituent parts obscured and even distorted the full meaning of that behaviour (Child, 1981). Along with Kohler and Koffka, he founded the school of Gestalt psychology which focused on the study of perception as a means of understanding learning.

The most important contribution of the Gestalt psychologists was their study of insight. 'Insightful' learning, they contested, occurs as a sudden solution to a problem in a way that can be readily be repeated during a similar event in the future, and which can be transferred to new situations.

Kohler's first demonstration of insightful learning, and one which best helps to describe it, used chimpanzees as subjects. Bananas were placed out of reach of chimpanzees in a cage. The chimpanzees were provided with two short sticks, neither of which was long enough to reach the bananas. When slotted together, however, the bananas could be reached easily. Similarly, some of the bananas were suspended from the roof of the cage, and could not be reached unless two or more of the boxes (also provided) were used as steps. In both of these cases, some of the chimpanzees suddenly 'had the idea' about how to solve the problem. This sudden, immediate, repeatable and transposable behaviour is how Kohler defined insight. Hergenhahn (1988) defines insight as an 'aha' experience similar to that which usually takes place within an observer on discovering the pictorial representation of a 'hidden' bear pictured in Figure 2.1.

Figure 2.1. Can you find the hidden bear?

Source: Munn et al., 1972: p.164

According to Gestalt theory, therefore, learning is a cognitive phenomenon. The learner, whether chimpanzee or human, comes to 'see' the solution after pondering a problem. The learner thinks about the ingredients necessary to solve a problem and puts them together in different ways until the problem is solved. Of key importance is that the problem can only exist in two states, unsolved or solved: there is no state of partial solution in between. Whereas the Behaviourists believed that learning was *continuous* (in that it increased systematically in small amounts), the Gestalt theorists believed learning was *discontinuous,* because a solution is either reached or it is not.

Hergenhahn (1988: p.257) summarizes four key characteristics of insightful learning:

1. The transition from pre-solution to solution is sudden and complete.

2. The performance based upon a solution gained by insight is usually smooth and free from errors.

3. A solution to a problem gained by insight is retained for a considerable length of time.

4. A principle gained by insight is easily adapted to other problems.

The Gestalt theorists also recognised 'the whole as being more than the sum of its parts — that to dissect is to distort' (Hergenhahn, 1988: p.244). This is based on the belief that psychological experiences are different from sensory experiences, although the former may result from the latter. In one of Wertheimer's early experiments, two lights blink on and off at a certain rate giving the observer the impression that one light is moving back and forth. The illusion of motion is a 'phenomonological experience' different from the sensory experience of two blinking lights. In the same way, the experience of listening to a symphony is more than the sum of the notes being played by members of the orchestra.

2.3.4 Consensus

Reflecting on the wide variations of the theories of learning outlined above, there is, as Smith (1983: p.34) notes, 'perhaps only one common feature: newness. Something that did not exist or was not grasped has been manifested or brought to life'.

Clearly, there is no complete agreement about the details of learning. Child (1981) observes, nevertheless, that whilst no single theory accounts for all the facts there is a basic premise accepted by most psychologists that learning occurs whenever new behaviour is adopted — or existing behaviour modified — to the extent that it has an influence on future performance or attitudes. Unless there were, in fact, some influence, it would not be possible to detect that learning had taken place. This change in behaviour, Child maintains, grows out of past experience and is distinguished from behaviour which results from simply 'growing up'.

2.4. Principles of learning

According to Hartley (1998), the relationship between learning theory and education in practice is a symbiotic one: theory contributes to practice, and practice contributes to theory. Because of this, he observes, there has been a swing over the past two decades against earlier theories, particularly Skinner's theories of operant conditioning. Whilst recognising that operant conditioning and reinforcement still play an important part in human learning, he rejects the notion that human learners are merely passive recipients of instruction in favour of the view that 'learners are active processors of information using a variety of strategies to remember and utilise knowledge (strategies which they can switch on and off in different contexts), and that learners are very flexible.' (p.16). This view is also held by leading distance learning authors and is discussed further in Chapter 3.

Hartley (1998) has developed a concise series of learning *principles* which is of particular relevance to the adult learner and is based around the theories of learning outlined above. These are summarized in Boxes 2.1 to 2.3. Whilst acknowledging that there is an overlap, he forms three groups of principles, as emphasized in *behavioural psychology*; *cognitive psychology*; and what he calls *social and phenomenological psychology*.

Box 2.1.

Principles of learning emphasized in behavioural psychology

These focus on the effects of the consequences of doing something on the subsequent repetition of that behaviour. Reinforced activities increase, non-reinforced activities decline. For learning, emphasis is placed on external events and the acquisition of responses and habits.

Key principles:

- **Activity is important.** Learning is likely to be enhanced when the learner is active rather than passive.

- **Repetition, generalization and discrimination are key concepts** (implying that frequent practice is necessary for learning to take place).

- **Reinforcement is the main motivating force.** The effects of the consequences on subsequent behaviour are important, whether extrinsic (reward from a teacher) or intrinsic (self-reward). It is generally found that positive reinforcers (rewards, successes) are to be preferred to negative events (punishments, failures).

- **Learning is enhanced when objectives are clear.** Behavioural objectives state what it is that the learner will be expected to be able to do at the end of the learning session. These expectations are usually expressed in terms of behaviours that can be measured. To achieve these objectives, tasks are often broken down into carefully sequenced stages following a task analysis.

Source: After Hartley, 1998: pp.17-18

Box 2.2.

Principles of learning emphasized in cognitive psychology

These focus on internal events. Learning results from inferences, expectations and making connections. Learners acquire plans and strategies.

Key principles:

- **Instruction should be well structured and well organized.** There should be logical relationships between key ideas and concepts: material which is well organized is easier to learn and remember.

- **Perceptual features of tasks are important.** Learners are selective to different features of their learning environment, so the way in which problems are presented to learners is important.

- **Prior knowledge is important.** For learners to acquire something new, it must fit with what they already know.

- **Differences between individuals are important to recognize.** As well as the differences in intellectual ability and personality, differences in 'cognitive style' or methods of approach also affect learning.

- **Learning with understanding is better than learning by rote** (without understanding).

Source: After Hartley, 1998: pp.18-19

Box 2.3.

Principles emphasized in social and phenomenological psychology

These focus on emotions and experience. Knowledge is gained by living, and experience is defined by 'what is in the head' rather than 'what is out there'.

Key principles:

- **Learning is a natural process.** Curious by nature, people have a propensity for learning and cannot stop.

- **Social situations affect learning.** Learning is rarely an isolated event. The group atmosphere of learning, whether it is competitive, co-operative, democratic, and valued by the group will affect the success and satisfaction of learning.

- **The purposes and goals of learning are important** as they provide important motivators for learning and the setting of future goals.

- **Choice, relevance and responsibility** are important factors in learning. Learning is enhanced when material for learning is personally relevant and when learners are responsible for their own learning. Significant learning only takes place when learners choose what they want to learn, how they want to learn it, and when they want to learn it (Holt, 1982).

- **Learning best takes place in a realistic setting** rather than in abstract and decontextualized situations.

- **Individuals and groups of people are key sources of knowledge.**

- **Discussions which emphasize meaningful explanations about learning are important.**

- **Self-assessment is an important skill.**

- **Learning involves conceptual changes,** not just the acquisition of new knowledge.

- **Anxiety and emotion affect learning.** Learning is not just a cognitive process. Learning that involves emotion as well as intellect is often the most lasting and pervasive.

Source: After Hartley, 1998: pp.20-21

2.5. Individual differences and learning styles

Boxes 2.1 to 2.3 provide a comprehensive list of learning principles. The significance of individual differences and learning styles is worth emphasizing, as it is a particularly important issue in adult education.

It has long been apparent to teachers, educators and observers that adults differ in how they go about certain activities associated with learning. There are differences in how people think, and in how people process information. Some people prefer to 'get the big picture' of the subject first, and then build towards full understanding. Others prefer to begin with details and examples. The 'big picture' emerges in the process. Likewise, some people prefer theory before practice, while others prefer to attach theory to experience (Smith, 1983).

Learners are often categorized more formally as either 'activists', 'reflectors', 'theorists', or 'pragmatists' according to their learning styles and approaches to problem-solving. Shaw (2000) profiles these as follows:

The activist:
- faces the challenge of a new problem;
- 'gets stuck in', has a go and tries things out;
- enjoys excitement, dramas and crises;
- enjoys the 'limelight'; and
- generates ideas and solves problems as part of a team.

Activists, therefore, will have creative ideas and will not necessarily be held back by practical considerations. They will respond well to new and novel ideas, complete tasks with instant rewards which make them good 'starters'. They will be sociable working in a team and force working relationships which may develop into friendships. On the other hand, they may be overpowering in a group and make others feel inferior. Their interest in problems and analysis tend to be limited which can make them poor 'finishers'.

The reflector:

- likes to stand back from, observe and consider problems;
- prefers time to think before taking action;
- will carry out research to gather relevant information pertaining to the problem; and
- communicates best when dialogue takes place within a structured environment.

Reflectors think first and then act, and so can be tactful and sensitive in group situations. They are good observers and, with consideration, are able to make sound evaluations. Decisions are likely to be well researched and resulting actions appropriate. Reflectors take time, however, limiting opportunities for trying out alternative ideas. They may be intimidated by activists who, enjoying the limelight, are quick to pick up and drop their ideas.

The theorist:

- likes to explore systems, theories and concepts;
- questions methodology and appreciates difficult and searching questions;
- likes a clear purpose, is rational and logical in approach to problems; and
- will pursue interesting ideas, even though they may not appear to be immediately relevant.

Theorists gain understanding by studying in detail. They are able to evaluate by analysis and make predictions from their knowledge. Decisions will be based on reason and logic rather than emotions and feelings. They can, however, pay too much attention to detail and not empathize with people of lesser intellectual ability. They would not join in a group unless they knew what they were doing and why.

The pragmatist:

- sees the links between the subject matter and a problem;
- will follow instructions when there are obvious practical benefits;
- will respond to coaching and feedback;
- enjoys 'real' problems; and
- concentrates on practical issues and develops action plans which lead to an obvious goal.

Pragmatists are well prepared, practical and reliable, and are always looking for improvements and better working practices. Understanding the practical before becoming involved, however, can be limiting.

Few people, of course, fall wholly within any of the four groups described above. Most can, at times, display tendencies from all groups. There are personality tests available which attempt to determine to what extent an individual is either an activist, reflector, theorist or pragmatist. Nevertheless, consideration of these tendencies as groups is a potent reminder of the diversity of the human personality in respect to both problem solving specifically, and learning in general.

2.6. Adult education

The theories and principles of learning, individual differences and learning styles have clear implications for adult education. Before discussing these, however, it is worth establishing what is meant by 'adult education' within the context of this research.

2.6.1 What is adult education?

The term 'adult education' is generally used in three ways. Firstly, it is used to describe a process through which people continue to learn after formal schooling ceases and which may take various forms. The second is to refer to the organized activities that institutions and agencies provide for adults. The third is to convey the idea of a field of social practice (Smith, 1983).

Other terms such as 'continuing education' and 'lifelong learning' are often used instead of 'adult education' which can carry negative connotations of remedial activity in, for example, literacy and numeracy. Throughout this research, however, 'adult education' refers to positive educational activities which prepare professionals for career development. The term 'adult', in itself, is a broad one and refers here to anyone who has assumed the general responsibilities associated with adulthood, such as working or parenting, or who is simply responsible for his or her own life. This usually means anyone over the age of eighteen.

2.6.2 Four characteristics of adult learners

The literature concerning adult education contains much information about the nature of adult learners, how they differ from children and teenagers as learners and the implications of this in practice.

Smith (1983: pp.38-47) describes four critical key characteristics of adult learners:

- They have a different orientation to education and learning.
- They have an 'accumulation of experience'.
- They display 'special development trends'.
- They are 'anxious and ambivalent' about learning.

2.6.2.1 Orientation to education and learning

Most children growing up in the West usually spend their time at play or at school. Adults, on the other hand, have multiple tasks, responsibilities and opportunities. They are free to choose to participate in education and bring with them a special orientation to learning that arises out of their perception of time as finite. Kidd (1973: p.48) describes their condition in this way:

'Adults have more stable interests and a different perception of time. They are able to internalize long-range goals and work toward them over a period of time. On the other hand, many adults, as well as youth, live in the here and now and will seldom work toward distant goals unless they themselves have a commitment to these goals. To the old, what time is left may appear very short, and to be valued rather than spent...

For an adult, more than for a child, the investment of time in an activity may be as important a decision as the investment of money or effort.'

According to Kidd (1973: p.49), the perception of life as an 'ever-increasing past, a fleeting, pressured present, and a finite future' may drive adults towards or away from education. It exerts pressure for resolving conflicts and solving problems but it also 'involves conflicting concerns, needs and desires which can become essential content in the learning process.'

2.6.2.2 Accumulation of experience

Adults approach education with experience unavailable to the child. Furthermore, 'much of this experience is qualitatively different to that of children. It derives from a wide range of roles and responsibilities. ... The accumulated experience usually includes many events of impact and stress. Adults are apt to have the foundation of their lives stripped away from time to time.' (Smith, 1983: p.40).

Davis and McCallon, (1975: p.26) describe this process in this way:

'The college dorm is not the same as the room back home. Leisurely afternoons are burned away by the new born baby. Jobs are lost. Parents die. Ideals are tarnished. Divorces occur. Bodies don't perform as they once did. Children leave home. The stock market crashes. Responsibilities are taken away. Retirement becomes mandatory. Mates die and leave them alone.'

Despite the many similarities in adult roles and responsibilities, Smith notes that the sum of each person's experiences leads to differences in values and beliefs and in ways of reacting to new information. Knox (1977) observes that representative samples of adults in their fifties are more varied in learning ability than representative samples of those in their twenties. Although the members of the groups appear to be quite similar, they are actually more heterogeneous than a group of children. That adults are in many ways unique affects preferences for modes of learning and learning environments which partly forms the basis for the learning style concept described above.

The significant role of past experience in the learning process of adults is clear to see from these observations. Ausubel (1968) maintains that it is what the learner already knows that is *the most important* factor which influences learning. Brundage and MacKeracher (1980: pp.32-33) summarize what happens in the adult learning process:

'Past experience … determines what information will be selected for further attention and how it will be interpreted; and determines what meanings, values, strategies, and skills will be employed first. If these are found to be suitable, new learning will proceed efficiently and productively. If these are found to be unsuitable, the adult will first search back through all previous experience for some suitable material which can be applied indirectly. If nothing can be found, the adult is faced with a considerable challenge: to acknowledge the inadequacy of meanings, values, and strategies.'

If this challenge is too difficult for the learner to confront, then the learner may well reject the 'validity, value and necessity of learning anything' (ibid.). Past experience, therefore, whilst it can be the base for new learning, can also be an obstacle which discourages learning. Smith (1983) believes that it often requires 'unlearning': i.e. helping adults to examine established meanings, values, skills and strengths, and to proceed to a new awareness and to new insight about themselves as learners.

Smith (1983: p.42) also notes that there is an additional effect of the adults accumulation of experience which is 'to make adult learners themselves very important resources for learning. They can often direct their own learning and learn a great deal from each other.'

2.6.2.3 *Special development trends*

Here, the term 'development' refers to changes in personal characteristics and attitudes. Studies in adult development have revealed that adults pass through developmental phases that are different from those experienced by pre-adults. During periods of transition following major life changes, for example, adults can appear receptive to education and learning related to reassessing personal goals, reasserting themselves as valued members of society, and reconfirming self-esteem (Smith, 1983: p.43). Aslanian and Brickell (1980) sampled 2000 people over the age of twenty-five and found 83 per cent of them learning in order to cope with a life change. According to Smith, periods of transition trigger learning in three major ways:

1. A change in life circumstances which occurs unexpectedly may require learning in order to adapt to the new situation.

2. Slower transitions may allow more comfortable accommodation to change by stimulating learning as the transition occurs.

3. After a period of life review, adults may choose to make changes and prepare for these through anticipatory learning (McCoy, 1980: p.76).

2.6.2.4 *Anxiety and ambivalence about learning*

Adults typically confront educational opportunity and participate in learning with mixed feelings and even with fear (Smith, 1983). Life changes produce stress which can be harmful in excess. Learning itself is an active process, and there may be some discomfort, even pain, in giving up that which has become comfortable. Learning can demand a 'temporary surrender of security' (Sheehy, 1976). Even when the decision to engage in learning is voluntary, changes in thoughts, attitudes and values can induce anxiety which may be exaggerated by doubts about learning potential and ability. Knox (1977) notes that capacities tend to be underestimated and underused.

During a period of crisis when the ego is already under stress, fear and anxiety may be highest (Smith, 1983). A major effect of anxiety is distraction from the learning tasks because our faculties are put to work mobilizing personal defences (McKinley, 1978). When stress is high, adults can find it difficult to communicate in learning situations, some displaying 'high oral communication apprehension' and try to avoid oral communication altogether (McCrosky and Anderson, 1976).

An area of ambivalence which affects education and learning concerns autonomy. Adults have deep-seated needs to move toward autonomy and self-direction. Normal adult development involves a gradual increase in personal willingness to take responsibility for guiding one's life based on values and ideas chosen by oneself (Fales and Greey, 1981). As adults strive for independence, however, there is also a need for approval and support of others. Smith (1983: p.45) observes that when adult learners have too little autonomy, 'their dignity can be affronted, their motivation inhibited and their pleasure in learning stifled. But learners suddenly confronted with more responsibility for their own learning than they expected, or are used to, usually respond with anxiety, and sometimes withdrawal.'

2.6.3 Optimum conditions for adult learning

Learners, therefore, require a learning environment that minimizes anxiety and fosters confidence. While some tension is normal, even desirable for seeking out learning potential and stimulating personal challenges, there is also a need to avoid extreme stress which can produce negative effects. Smith (1983) cites six optimum conditions for learning which are of particular relevance to adult learners. These are presented in Box 2.4.

Box 2.4. Optimum conditions for learning

Adults learn best when these six conditions are met:

1. They feel the need to learn and have input into what, why, and how they will learn.

2. The content and processes of learning bear a perceived and meaningful relationship to past experience and experience is used as a resource for learning.

3. What is to be learned relates to the individual's developmental changes and life tasks.

4. The amount of autonomy exercised by the learner is congruent with that required by the mode or method of learning.

5. They learn in a climate that minimizes anxiety and encourages freedom to experiment.

6. Their learning styles are taken into account.

Source: Smith, 1983: pp.47-49

2.7. 'The professional' as adult learner

It is clear that adults learn in different ways to pre-adults, but they also learn in different ways to each other, depending on the amount and nature of their experience.

The most obvious way of classifying adult learning groups is by age. Common divisions are: early adulthood: 18 to 39; middle adulthood: 40 to 59; and later adulthood: 60 upwards. Smith (1983), however, describes four 'special populations' which do not necessarily correspond with these age groups. These populations are 'the undereducated; those returning to college; the professional; and the older person'.

Definition and analysis of the 'professional' as adult learner is given here, as this population is the focus of the research reported and discussed in Part II.

Smith (1983: pp.51-52) believes that professional people are likely to have relatively high incomes, access to resources, and a variety of life-styles. He suggests that they are most likely as a group to continue their education; they are better established in their communities; and they are more mobile, and more confident in their abilities (including the ability to learn) than a cross-section of the general population. He also observes that they feel heavily pressed for time, as their careers absorb a great deal of their time and energy. Pre-professional education may have left professional learners ill-equipped as a result of its emphasis on authoritative presentation of information, and encouragement of dependency relationships with teachers.

Smith also argues that while few professionals doubt their own learning ability, their participation and learning are affected by the need to avoid revealing professional competence in public. With regard to the role of experience in learning, the professional possesses a technical vocabulary and specialized frames of reference for relating new information to old. That same experience base can be a handicap in learning for other than job-related purposes.

Smith believes the professional can be expected to have adequate levels of cognitive development for most learning endeavours, but when it comes to involving professionals in planning and evaluative processes, obstacles arise. These learners are usually capable of meaningful involvement, but they may feel that time pressures and the need for precise, problem-centred information make it necessary for authorities to diagnose needs, set the objectives, and determine the learning activities for continuing education programmes.

So professionals tend to be in possession of the tools for learning, to undertake considerable learning on their own, but are wary of opportunities for input into processes, especially where job-related learning is concerned. Collaborative learning is not as appealing (and perhaps appropriate) for them as the traditional and self-directed modes.

The following chapter looks at these ideas in more detail, focusing on the learning requirements of the 'international development professional'.

Chapter 3

International Development and Distance Learning

3.1. Introduction

This chapter examines the ways in which self-directed modes of learning, and in particular distance learning, can support the education and training needs of the professional adult as described in the previous chapter. It focuses on the needs of professionals whose work is involved with development in low- and middle-income countries.

The chapter begins with a discussion of the goal of international development and the need for education and training to realize this goal. It describes conventional teaching methods, and goes on to outline the distance learning alternative and the benefits and problems of this approach. It also examines ways of delivering distance learning programmes, focusing in particular on print-based materials. The chapter concludes with an examination of some of the ways in which distance learning is being used in low- and middle-income countries, especially in engineering and infrastructure development.

3.2. The goal of international development

Internationally agreed targets have been set to halve the proportion of people living in abject poverty by 2015, together with associated targets including universal access to primary education and basic education by the same date (DFID, 1998).

29

However optimistic these targets may appear, the goal of international development to improve the health, well-being and livelihood opportunities of the world's poorest communities is, nevertheless, a common aspiration. Realizing this aspiration depends, to a large extent, on the successful implementation of sustainable development projects and programmes. This requires collaboration across a range of professions, and the formation of partnerships between governments, the private sector and civil society (ibid.).

3.3. The education and training needs of development professionals

There continues to be a clear need for education and training to support development initiatives at all levels, not least for the practitioners who bridge the gap between communities and external support agencies (see Figure 3.1). It is education and training at this level, with a particular emphasis on the provision of infrastructure, which is considered here, but it should be emphasised that education and training at *all* levels is essential for development to be effective and sustainable.

Figure 3.1. A role for education and training in supporting development

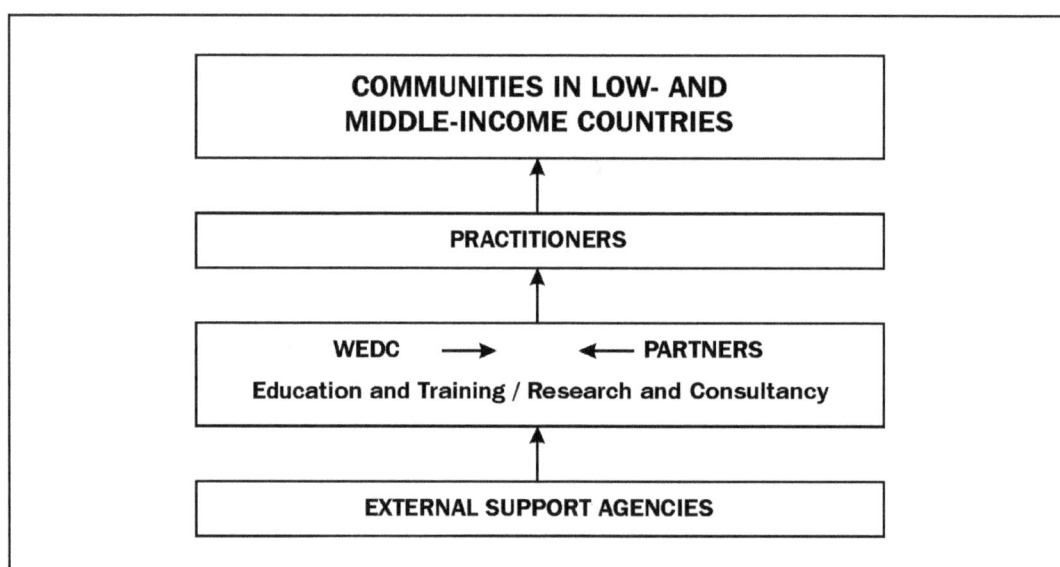

Source: Smout, 1996

The primary aims of education and training are to encourage learning and to advance understanding. For development professionals concerned with planning, providing and managing physical infrastructure, this means upgrading knowledge, skills and attitudes necessary to enable them to become technically competent, managerially skilled, consumer and community aware, environmentally sensitive and commercially adept (Franceys, 1996). They also require recognition of their experience, status and individual needs; a learning environment which provides support and reinforces motivation; and an award of academic qualifications which enhances their career prospects (ibid.).

Progressive academic institutions understand the principles of learning as outlined in Chapter 1, and recognize that choice and flexibility of education and training programmes best serves the needs of development professionals. These programmes can range from short, intensive courses to longer programmes at graduate and postgraduate levels. Teaching methods may be varied, and include lectures and presentations; interactive teaching; group work; case studies and simulations; practical work; and the preparation of individual research projects. All these can encourage participants to apply new thinking from their courses to their work situations, and develop analytical skills and new attitudes which are essential for lasting change (Smout, 1996).

3.4. Meeting education and training needs: The distance learning alternative

Distance learning is an alternative means of reaching out to potential learners who have the education and training needs described above, but who are not able to attend conventional programmes. The following discussion presents the benefits and the problems of this approach, beginning with a definition of what is meant by 'distance learning' within the context of this thesis.

3.4.1 A definition of distance learning

Rowntree (1990; 1994) offers the most appropriate definition, describing distance learning as a form of self-instruction that caters for learners who are learning, quite literally, at a distance — i.e. those who will not be in regular contact with the teachers who design the courses. Correspondence education is a typical example of distance learning. Other examples include the use of materials 'on-site' (sometimes collectively with other learners) such as on the premises of an institution sponsoring the course. This is often referred to as 'flexible learning', 'open learning' or 'mixed-mode learning'.

On-site distance learners may still see little or nothing of the developers of the course but may have the advantage of meeting with colleagues and perhaps a tutor or adviser. Willis (1993) also notes that, at its most basic level, distance education takes place when teacher and student are separated by physical distance, but that it can also take place 'in concert with face-to-face communication'. There is also the 'non-physical' concept of distance, however, which refers to the gap in social and cultural outlook of particular learning groups.

Whether studying on-site or alone, on-line or from paper-based materials, all distance learners rely heavily on specially prepared materials, i.e. instruction which is pre-planned and pre-packaged (Rowntree, 1990).

3.4.2 Educational implications

From an educational perspective (as opposed to administrative or logistical perspectives), there are both benefits and problems associated with learning at a distance. These are closely related to the principles of learning outlined in Chapter 2, and concern learners and programme developers and tutors alike. The following discussion highlights some of the main issues.

3.4.2.1 *Meeting specific needs*

Meeting the education and training needs of students is the cornerstone of every effective education and training programme, including distance learning programmes. Regardless of the educational context, the primary role of the student is to learn. This is a daunting and complex task under the best of circumstances, requiring motivation, planning, and an ability to analyse and apply the instructional content of the programme. When instruction is delivered at a distance, additional challenges result because students are often separated from others sharing their backgrounds and interests.

Willis (1995) notes that it can be more difficult for teachers to meet the specific needs of distance learners than it is to meet the needs of learners in a classroom situation because classroom teachers rely on a number of visual and unobtrusive cues from their students to enhance their delivery of instructional content. He suggests that a quick glance, for example, reveals who is attentively taking notes, pondering a difficult concept, or preparing to make a comment. It can be equally apparent if a student is frustrated, confused, tired, or simply bored. The attentive teacher consciously and subconsciously receives and analyses these visual cues and adjusts the course delivery to meet the needs of the class during a particular session.

In contrast, the distant teacher has few, if any, visual cues. Even with video conferencing, it is still difficult, according to Willis, to carry on a stimulating teacher-class discussion when spontaneity is altered by technical requirements. The teacher might never really know, for example, if students are asleep, talking among themselves or even in the room.

Nevertheless, research comparing distance education to traditional face-to-face instruction indicates that teaching and studying at a distance can be as effective as traditional instruction when the method and technologies used are appropriate to

33

the instructional tasks, there is student-to-student interaction, and when there is timely teacher-to-student feedback (Moore et al., 1990; Verduin and Clark, 1991).

Teaching and learning at a distance are demanding. Learning, however, will be more meaningful and 'deeper' for distant students, if students and their tutors share responsibility for developing learning goals and objectives; if tutors actively interact with class members, promote reflection on experience, relate new information to examples that make sense to learners; and if students maintain their self-esteem and evaluate what is being learned. This is the challenge and the opportunity provided by distance education (Willis, 1995).

3.4.2.2 Performance

There is some evidence to suggest that performance of students on project work and continuous assessment is generally better for distance learning students than for those on full-time courses. Learners can apply newly-acquired skills to their work as soon as they are gained which enhances both work performance and learning because it is focussed on 'real-life' scenarios and on the experience of the learner (Bilham and Gilmour, 1995).

The high-level of interactivity between learner and course material which forms part of the best examples of distance learning also produces better long-term retention of knowledge and skills (ibid.). Achievement on various tests administered by course instructors tends to be higher for distant as opposed to conventional students (Souder, 1993).

Some research suggests that distance learners bring basic characteristics to their learning experience which influence their success in coursework. Such learners are voluntarily seeking further education; have post-secondary education goals with expectations for higher grades; are highly motivated and self-disciplined; and are older (Schlosser and Anderson, 1994).

Other studies conclude that there are a number of factors which determine successful learning whether or not students are studying at a distance. These include a willingness to initiate contact with tutors for assistance; having a serious attitude toward the course or programme; employment in a field where career advances can be readily achieved by upgrading academic qualifications; and the previous completion of a university or college degree (Ross and Powell, 1990; Bernt and Bugbee, 1993).

Taking graduation rates as a measure of success, Young et al. (1991) believe there is enough evidence to assert that it compares reasonably well with other forms of part-time education, even though fewer students at distance teaching institutions successfully complete their courses than those studying face-to-face. Australian experience suggests that graduation rates for off-campus students studying at a distance are comparable to those of part-time students studying conventionally on campus.

3.4.2.3 *Group learning*

Learners benefit significantly from their involvement in small learning groups. These groups provide support and encouragement along with extra feedback on course assignments. Most importantly, groups can foster the feeling that help, if needed, is readily available (Willis, 1995).

Group learning is generally perceived to be difficult at a distance. Although distance learners can be encouraged to communicate and learn from one another by making available names and contact details to all members of the learning group, simply living in different communities and geographic regions deprives the teacher and students of a common community link. The opportunities for 'multi-way' communication (as opposed to one-way or two-way communication) are considerably reduced. Setting up computer user groups may provide some opportunities for group communication, but this is technology-dependent and excludes those learners who may not have access to the Internet or other computer networks. Besides, the very nature of a 'virtual' group differs from that of a physical group. Less confident members may never contribute to an on-line discussion. A skilled facilitator of a physical group, on the other hand, is more likely to encourage contributions from all members. Learning as part of a group is a motivating force. Without the support of peers, some learners can become dispirited and even withdraw from a programme of study.

3.4.2.4 Support, feedback and interaction

Although procedures can be put in place to facilitate the smooth administration of distance learning course applications and enrolment, communication difficulties can lengthen the time it takes to give and receive feedback. On-site learners are likely to have more opportunities for in-depth appraisal of their work as it progresses.

Many learners require support and guidance to make the most of their distance learning experiences This support typically takes the form of some combination of student-tutor and student-student interaction (Threlkeld and Brzoska, 1994).

Other research findings concerning the need for interaction have produced some important guidelines for distance learning tutors:

- Learners value timely feedback regarding course assignments, exams, and projects (Egan et al., 1991).

- Learners are more motivated if they are in frequent contact with the instructor. More structured contact might be used as a motivational tool (Coldeway et al., 1980).

- Use of on-site facilitators who develop a personal rapport with students and who are familiar with equipment and other course materials increases student satisfaction with courses (Burge and Howard, 1990).

- The use of technologies such as fax machines, computers, and telephones can also provide learner support and interaction opportunities (Willis, 1995).

3.4.2.5 Flexible study

Distance learning provides opportunities for study for those disadvantaged, not only by distance, but also by limited time or physical disability. It is a flexible form of study. The proliferation in recent years of all kinds of distance learning programmes is proof enough of their appeal. Promotional brochures usually cite the following in some form as ways of attracting learners to a particular course of study:

- **Flexibility of place** means that study is not confined to a particular location. There is the potential for study to be undertaken anywhere in the world (WEDC, 2000).

- **Flexibility of time** allows learners to study at the most convenient times of day or week allowing those in employment to continue in their jobs, and those engaged in child care to remain with their families (ibid). In view of the home-based role of many women in developing countries, it is especially appropriate as a means of education and training (Bilham and Gilmour, 1995).

- **Flexibility of pace** allows learners to control the rate of study, to study part-time or full-time for example — or to concentrate on particular areas of interest (WEDC, 2000).

- **Flexibility of content and delivery.** Distance learning tends to be delivered in a modular form which can allow learners to devise their own programmes of study based on a range of subjects. This method better accommodates systems for credit accumulation and transfer (ibid.).

- **Accessibility.** Distance learning offers accessible training to students living in rural areas (ibid.).

- **Cost-effectiveness.** Students may complete their course of study without suffering the loss of salary due to relocation (ibid.).

3.4.2.6 Learning resources

Although many distance learning programmes provide adequate resources for learners to undertake a course of study, few will be able to take into account the full diversity of learners' interests. Access to library resources for some learners may be difficult and in many cases impossible. Internet-based programmes can overcome some of these difficulties, but this currently reduces the opportunities of participation for the many potential learners who live in low- and middle-income countries.

3.4.2.7 Effective instruction

Good distance teaching practices are fundamentally identical to good conventional teaching practices. Those factors which influence good instruction are universal across different environments and populations (Wilkes and Burnham, 1991). Because distance education and its technologies require extensive planning and preparation, distance educators must consider the following in order to improve their effectiveness (Schlosser and Anderson, 1994):

- Extensive pre-planning and formative evaluation is necessary. Distance learners value instructors who are well prepared and organized (Egan et al., 1991).

- Learners benefit significantly from a well-designed syllabus. Structured note taking, using tools such as interactive study guides, and the use of visuals and graphics as part of the syllabus and study outlines contribute to student understanding of the course. Such visuals, however, must be tailored to the characteristics of the medium and to the characteristics of the students (ibid.).

3.4.2.8 Learning how to learn at a distance

The primary role of the student is to learn. Under the best of circumstances, this challenging task requires motivation, planning, and the ability to analyse and apply the information being taught. In a distance education setting, the process of student learning is more complex for several reasons (Schuemer, 1993):

- Many distance-education students are older, have jobs, and families. They must co-ordinate the different areas of their lives which influence each other — their families, jobs, spare time, and studies.

- Distance learners have a variety of reasons for taking courses. Some students are interested in obtaining a degree to qualify for a better job. Many take courses to broaden their education and are not really interested in a formal qualification.

- In distance education, the learner is usually isolated. The motivational factors arising from the contact or competition with other students is absent. The student also lacks the immediate support of a teacher who is present and able to motivate and, if necessary, give attention to actual needs and difficulties that occur during study.

- Distance learners and their tutors often have little in common in terms of background and day-to-day experiences and it therefore takes longer for learner-tutor rapport to develop. Without face-to-face contact, distance learners may feel ill at ease with their tutor as an individual and uncomfortable with their learning situation.

New distance learners may have some difficulty determining what the demands of a course of academic study actually are because they do not have the support of an immediate peer group, ready access to the instructor, or in some cases, familiarity with the technology being used for delivery of the distance learning course. They may be unsure of themselves and their learning. Morgan (1991) suggests that distance learners who are not confident about their learning tend to concentrate on memorizing facts and details in order to complete assignments and write exams. As a result, they end up with a poor understanding of course material. He views memorization of facts and details as a 'surface approach' to learning. Learners who adopt this approach will focus on the text or instruction itself rather than on their intended learning outcomes; focus on discrete elements; memorize information and procedures for tests; associate concepts and facts without reflection; fail to distinguish principles from evidence, new information from old; treat assignments as something imposed by the instructor; and focus on the demands of assignments and exams leading to a knowledge that may be removed from everyday experience.

According to Morgan (1991), distance learners need to become more selective and focused in their learning in order to master new information. The focus of their learning needs to shift them from the surface approach to a 'deep approach'. Learners adopting a deep approach focus on the tutor's arguments; relate and distinguish new ideas and previous knowledge; relate concepts to everyday experience; relate and distinguish evidence and argument; organize and structure content; and focus on how instructional material relates to everyday reality. Surface and deep approaches to learning are also reported by Hartley (1998).

Shifting from 'surface' to 'deep' learning may take some time. Brundage, Keane, and Mackneson (1993) suggest that adult students and their instructors must face and overcome a number of challenges before learning takes place including: becoming and staying responsible for themselves; 'owning' their strengths, desires, skills, and needs; maintaining and increasing self-esteem; relating to others; clarifying what is learned; redefining what legitimate knowledge is; and dealing with content.

3.5. Delivering distance learning

As a result of the Information Technology (IT) revolution of the late twentieth century, a wide range of technological options are available to developers of distance learning programmes. They fall into four major categories:

Voice: Instructional audio tools include the interactive technologies of telephone, audio-conferencing, and short-wave radio. Passive (i.e. one-way) audio tools include tapes and radio.

Video: Instructional video tools include still images such as slides, pre-produced moving images (e.g. film, videotape), and real-time moving images combined with audio-conferencing (one-way or two-way video with two-way audio).

Computer-based: Computer applications for distance education are varied and include:

- Computer-assisted instruction (CAI) uses the computer as a self-contained teaching machine to present individual lessons.

- Computer-managed instruction (CMI) uses the computer to organize instruction and track student records and progress. The instruction itself need not be delivered via a computer, although CAI is often combined with CMI.

- Computer-mediated education (CME) describes computer applications that facilitate the delivery of instruction. Examples include electronic mail, fax, real-time computer conferencing, and World-Wide Web applications.

Print: Print-based materials founded distance learning and is the form of delivery from which all other delivery systems have evolved. Various print formats are available ranging from textbooks and study guides to workbooks, and case studies (see Section 3.5.2.3).

3.5.1 Appropriate methods of delivery

Research concerned with appropriate methods of delivering distance learning is varied. According to Martin and Rainey (1993), no significant difference in positive attitudes toward course material is apparent between distant and conventional education. According to Egan, et al. (1991), conventional instruction is perceived to be better organized and more clearly presented than instruction for distance education.

Other research indicates that the instructional format itself has little effect on student achievement as long as the delivery technology is appropriate to the content being offered and all participants have access to the same technology (Willis, 1995).

Willis (1995) recognizes that whilst technology can play a key role in the delivery of distance education, educators must remain focused on instructional outcomes, not the technology of delivery. The key to effective distance education is focusing on the needs of the learners, the requirements of the content, and the constraints faced by the tutor. Typically, he argues, this systematic approach will result in a mix of media, each serving a specific purpose. For example:

- A strong print component can provide much of the basic instructional content in the form of a course text, as well as readings, the syllabus, and day-to-day schedule.

- Interactive audio or video conferencing can provide real time face-to-face (or voice-to-voice) interaction. This is also an excellent and cost-effective way to incorporate guest speakers and content experts.

- Computer conferencing or electronic mail can be used to send messages, assignment feedback, and other targeted communication to one or more class members. It can also be used to increase interaction among students.

- Pre-recorded video tapes can be used to present class lectures and visually-oriented content.

- Fax machines can be used to distribute assignments and last minute announcements; to receive student assignments; and to provide timely feedback.

Using this integrated approach, Willis maintains, the educator's task is to carefully select among the technological options. The goal is to build a mix of instructional media, meeting the needs of the learner in a manner that is instructionally effective and economically prudent.

Whittington (1987) believes that future research should focus on the critical factor in determining student achievement: i.e. the design of instruction itself.

3.5.2 Print in distance education

The first distance-delivered courses were offered by correspondence study, with print materials sent and returned to students by mail. While technological developments have added to the repertoire of tools available to the distance educator, print continues to be a significant component of all distance education programmes. There are limitations with print, but also significant advantages (Willis, 1995).

3.5.2.1 Limitations of print

- **Print presents a limited view of reality.** Print, by its reliance on the written word, offers a vicarious view of reality. Despite the use of excellent sequential illustrations or photographs, for example, it is impossible to adequately recreate motion in print.

- **Print is passive and self-directed.** Numerous studies have shown that higher learner motivation is required to successfully complete print-based courses. To a certain extent, the passive nature of print can be offset by systematic instructional design that seeks to stimulate the passive learner. Nevertheless, it takes more motivation to read a book or work through a written exercise than it does to watch a television programme or participate in an audio-conference with an instructor encouraging student participation and response.

- **Print provides limited feedback and interaction.** Without feedback and interaction, instruction can suffer, regardless of the delivery system. Even with print materials incorporating feedback mechanisms and interactive exercises, it is easy for learners to skip to the answer sections.

- **Print demands high-levels of reading and language skills**. Print-based materials demand a high-level of reading skill, not only to understand subject specific language, but also to scan large quantities of material for selective study. Additional difficulties face those learners whose first language differs from the language in which the materials are written.

3.5.2.2 Advantages of print

- **Print is spontaneous.** Print materials can be used in any setting without the need for sophisticated presentation equipment.

- **Print is instructionally transparent.** The medium of delivery should enhance, not compete with, the content for the learner's attention. If the student reads well, the print medium is the most transparent instructional medium of all.

- **Print is non-threatening.** Reading is second nature to most professionals. As a result, they are easily able to focus on the content, without becoming frustrated by the process of reading itself.

- **Print is easy to use.** Given adequate light, print materials can be used at any time and at any place without the aid of supplemental resources such as electricity, a viewing screen, and specially-designed electronic classrooms. The portability of print is especially important for rural learners with limited access to advanced technology.

- **Print is easily reviewed and referenced.** Print materials are typically learner-controlled. As a result, the student rapidly moves through redundant sections, while focusing on areas demanding additional attention.

- **Print is cost-effective.** Print-based materials are usually cost-effective to produce and reproduce.

- **Print is easily edited and revised.** Compared with technically-sophisticated electronic software, print is both easy and inexpensive to edit and revise.

- **Print is time-effective.** When instructional print materials are created, the developer's primary focus remains on content concerns, not the technical requirements of the delivery system.

3.5.2.3 *Formats of print materials*

Various print formats are available, including:

- **Textbooks.** As conventionally delivered courses, textbooks are the basis and primary source of content for the majority of distance learning courses, and they are especially important when the learner and the instructor are not in daily contact.

- **Study guides.** Typically, distance educators use study guides to reinforce points made during class and through the use of other delivery systems. They will often include exercises, related readings and additional resources available to the student.

- **Workbooks.** In a distance education context workbooks are often used to provide course content in an interactive manner. Typical formats contain an overview, the content to be covered, one or more exercises or case studies to elaborate the points being made, and self-assessment tests with answers.

- **Case studies.** If written imaginatively, case studies are an extremely effective instructional tool. Case studies are often designed around the limitations of print and intended to inspire the imagination of students as they place themselves in particular 'real-life' situations. Many case studies present a content-based scenario. They raise questions, pose alternative solutions, and then lead students to different sections of the text where the consequences of the selected alternative are described.

3.5.2.4 *Designing instruction for print*

As print is largely a one-way communication medium, the challenge is to design instruction which maximizes the amount of interaction. The following sections are derived from guidelines drawn from Misanchuk (1994) and Rowntree (1990; 1994).

Writing style. Instructional materials should use language more like that used for speaking than for writing journal articles or books. It is best to use the active voice, personal pronouns, short sentences and familiar examples, and avoid using compound sentences, excess information, multiple negatives, jargon and unnecessary and difficult words and cultural and gender stereotyping.

Focusing on content organization before developing content. Prior to content development, it is essential to create an outline of the material to be covered. Print materials are often too 'wordy' because the author is planning, organizing and writing at the same time. Instead, it is preferable to organize content based on the identified goals and objectives. Initially, it is best to focus on systematically and creatively ordering the flow of topics, rather than 'polishing' a finished product. The end result will be a well-organized content outline from which the written content will easily flow.

Developing a course introduction. A written course introduction will usually be the first section a distance learner sees. The course introduction can include biographical background information about the instructor, a course overview, course goals and aims, a listing of any textbooks or additional learning materials that will be needed, and information about assignments, examinations, and grading.

Staying with a consistent format. Learner anxiety with the unknown can be reduced through consistency in instructional presentation. It is essential to develop an effective format and organizational scheme and then to 'stick with it'. Headings and subheadings will visually guide the reader through the material.

Using advance organizers. Advance organizers are a means of connecting new material with a learner's prior knowledge and cognitive structure. They should be of a more general and abstract character than the learning matter that follows and help the learner to relate different parts and concepts of teaching material to each other. It is best to place the most general and comprehensive ideas at the beginning of a lesson and progress to more structured and detailed information.

Using examples and analogies. In a traditional classroom, teachers spontaneously provide examples and analogies to illustrate a point that students are having difficulty understanding. Because distant students and their teachers may not have this type of interaction, including a number of good examples and analogies in print-based materials will be helpful. These examples should address the various cultural groups, ages and experiences of the students.

Including questions. Questions in print material can stimulate the learner to be more active and to deal more intensively with the learning matter. Questions that aim at understanding rather than merely reproduction and memorization of facts are preferable.

Adding a table of contents. A detailed table of contents can help the learner to quickly refer to the appropriate section.

Incorporating a glossary of terms. A glossary summarizes all the new, often technical terminology encountered in a document. It may be helpful to delineate glossary entries in the instructional material by putting them in boldface type.

3.6. Distance learning in low- and middle-income countries

3.6.1 History and background

Young et al. (1991) present a comprehensive review covering the use of distance learning for mass education in low- and middle income countries. In the second edition of *Distance Teaching for the Third World,* Young et al. describe the process of proliferation of distance learning institutions throughout the world.

Founded in 1969, the British Open University was one of the first and has evolved to become a respected partner of its conventional 'sister' universities.

'The idea was infectious, even as the world's economy was moving to recession. Open universities were established in Costa Rica and Venezuala, in Indonesia, Thailand and Japan, in Iran before the fall of the Shah and in Spain after the death of Franco. The People's Open University established by Bhutto in Pakistan became the Allama Iqbal Open University under Zia, survived the change and continues today. The Chinese Television University looks like being the largest educational institution in the world.'

(Young et al., 1991: pp.2)

Young et al. believe the existence of these distance learning institutions has changed the 'ecology' of distance education, the biggest change being one of scale. By 1991, The British Open University had become the country's second largest university. The Indonesian Open University had enrolled 65,000 students after a start-up period of only nine months.

The dramatic expansion of distance learning in developing countries was only due in part to the example of the British Open University. It was also a response to demand. The first Vice-Chancellor of the (then) People's Open University in Pakistan saw the university as …

'… entrusted with the task of serving the whole country and all categories of people … its clientele are the masses. It rejects the elitist view that only a selected class of people can benefit from higher education … that for any real learning to take place people have to be secluded behind the walls of educational institutions and pursue a rigidly structured curriculum. … Education for skilled labour, technicians and other occupations in business, industry and agriculture has mostly been ignored by the formal education system. The People's Open University will give high priority to the occupational education of farmers, industrial workers and craftsmen.'

(Zaki, 1975 in Young et al., 1991: pp.2)

For Zaki, as for others, distance education offered the chance to respond to public demand, to seek greater equity in education and to meet the needs for trained manpower. Different institutions have given varying emphasis to these three aims, but those in low- and middle-income countries have one thing in common: their students tend to be young. While in the North, distance teaching institutions have largely recruited students from adults seeking second-chance education, those in the South have to great a extent recruited from school-leavers who could not get to a full-time, conventional university (Young et al., 1991).

While the large countries of Asia established open universities as a national response to demands from a large population, African countries have operated on a more modest scale. The universities of Lagos, Nairobi and Zambia, for example, have distance teaching departments. Regional universities of the South Pacific and the West Indies have distance teaching units which are of particular significance for their scattered communities (ibid.).

3.6.2 Distance learning in engineering

An increasing number of distance learning programmes are concerned with international development. The particular focus of Part II is infrastructure development. This section reviews distance learning in engineering drawn from a report of the former Overseas Development Administration (ODA), now the Department for International Development (DFID) of the British Government.

In their report *Distance Education in Engineering for Developing Countries*, Bilham and Gilmour (1995) note that in developing and emerging countries where economic development is of fundamental importance, training for industrial growth is essential. Consequently, the initial education and the continuing professional development of engineers at all levels is paramount.

The report summarizes the findings of a major study carried out during 1994 involving a survey of the current provision of engineering distance education from the major providing countries. The study identified around 5,000 engineering distance education courses and 122 organizations listed in the UK as providers of engineering courses. Although the report does not identify those courses or programmes specifically designed to support development projects and programmes *per se*, it does focus on three countries, the Czech Republic, Sri Lanka and Zimbabwe. These case studies provide a useful insight into the important issues which relate to distance learning and development across a number of different sectors.

The study found that the issues related to engineering distance education were different in kind from non-technical education and could not easily be explained by text. The study also found a universal need in all three countries for updating in engineering, although the extent, level, subjects and immediacy of the need varied depending on the country.

The report also recognised that at the professional engineering level, numbers in individual countries requiring updating in any specific subject are smaller, so that the economies of scale brought about by distance education are less advantageous. In these cases, and where the training requirement is common, the report recommended that specialist courses should be produced or adapted and used to serve more than one country and that it would almost certainly be more cost-effective to buy in existing distance learning courses where possible. It also concluded that student support would be fundamental and where possible there should be a local tutor.

3.6.3 The WEDC distance learning programme

Bilham and Gilmour (1995) recognised that in the water engineering sector in Zimbabwe, distance learning could play a crucial role in providing necessary training at postgraduate level. At the same time there was recognition at the Water, Engineering and Development Centre (WEDC) that distance learning could play a wider role in international development taking account of the multi-disciplinary nature of development and the range of new skills required of development professionals. Following the example of Wye College which provides courses for the agricultural management sector, WEDC has developed five postgraduate modules for the water and environment sectors, with a particular emphasis on appropriate technology and management for infrastructure development in low-income communities. Additional modules leading to the accreditation of a MSc programme in Water and Environmental Management are planned.

3.6.4 The Global Distance Learning Network

The World Bank is currently in the process of establishing the Global Distance Learning Network (GDLN) intended to build on the World Bank Learning Network (WBLN) which has been in development since 1977. The WBLN uses interactive video, the Internet, and print media to facilitate the use of distance learning courses, teleseminars and special events from electronic classrooms in Washington DC. The World Bank's field offices now also serve as distance learning centres. In the long-term, it is intended the GDLN Distance Learning Centers will be owned and operated by training and educational institutions, independent of the Bank (World Bank, 2000).

Chapter 4

Information Design for Self-Instruction

4.1. Introduction

Information design is a broad discipline which impacts on many aspects of public life. Operation instructions for machinery, domestic appliances, road signs, maps and transport timetables are just a few examples of items which demand the professional attention of information designers.

One of the primary concerns of this research is the application of information design to instructional texts for learning — particularly distance learning for the development professional profiled in the previous chapters.

Chapter 4 defines what is meant by design for instruction and presents a review of the literature. Research into information design is carried out for many different reasons, which largely depend on the application of the design. Although this review is derived from literature concerning the design of paper-based learning materials, other research is referred to as appropriate. All of the literature considered here relates to materials which are printed in English.

4.2. Design and graphic design

Here, and in subsequent chapters, 'design' refers to both the structure of information *and* its visual characteristics. The more specific term 'graphic design' (or 'page design') refers to visual characteristics only.

The structure of information and how it looks, however, are closely linked. Figure 4.1 presents an overview of the process of designing a distance learning programme.

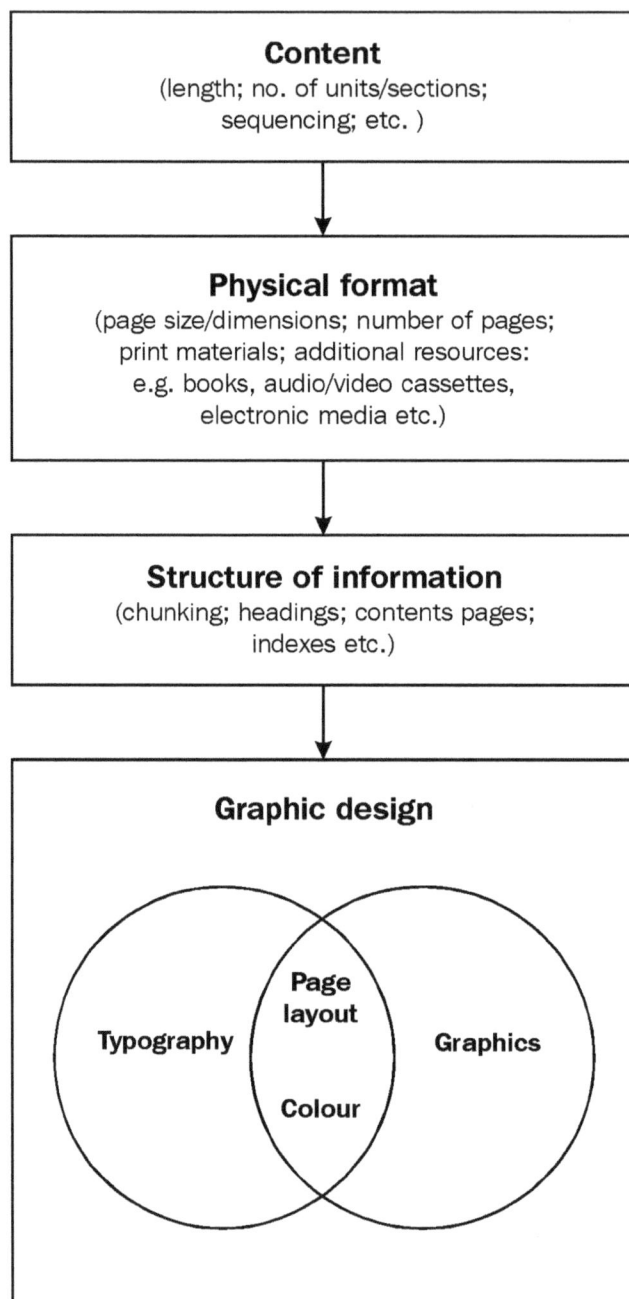

Figure 4.1. An overview of the process of designing a distance learning programme

```
┌─────────────────────────────────────────┐
│              Content                     │
│      (length; no. of units/sections;     │
│            sequencing; etc. )            │
└─────────────────────────────────────────┘
                    │
                    ▼
┌─────────────────────────────────────────┐
│           Physical format                │
│   (page size/dimensions; number of pages;│
│    print materials; additional resources:│
│      e.g. books, audio/video cassettes,  │
│           electronic media etc.)         │
└─────────────────────────────────────────┘
                    │
                    ▼
┌─────────────────────────────────────────┐
│         Structure of information         │
│    (chunking; headings; contents pages;  │
│             indexes etc.)                │
└─────────────────────────────────────────┘
                    │
                    ▼
┌─────────────────────────────────────────┐
│            Graphic design                │
│                                          │
│                Page                      │
│               layout                     │
│    Typography           Graphics         │
│                Colour                    │
│                                          │
└─────────────────────────────────────────┘
```

4.3. The structure of information

There has been a great deal of research undertaken concerning ways of organizing instructional text which reveals the underlying structure of the information it contains (Frase and Schwartz, 1979; Hartley, 1981; 1982). The premise for this research is that any layout that reveals structure will aid comprehension.

4.3.1 Chunking

Some research has concentrated on the effect of printing text so that each line contains only one meaningful unit. This is usually referred to as 'chunking' (Kempson and Moore, 1994), and is an extension of the notion of 'sense-lining' — a practice of printing each sentence or clause as a separate line rather than formatting text into a block without reference to its meaning. Sense-lining and chunking are usually reserved for reading literary works out aloud but has been seen to aid comprehension of other (particularly educational) texts.

Keenan (1984), however, suggests that the effects on legibility of variable line length that result from chunking counteracts the increase in comprehension.

4.3.2 Headings

There is considerable evidence to show that the use of headings to reveal the structure of information improves comprehension (Wright, 1979; Stark, 1988). Charrow and Redish, (1980) also note that the appropriate use of headings increases the likelihood of text being read in the first instance.

The value of headings depend on their position, their content and the way in which they are signalled (Wright, 1979). According to Hartley and Trueman (1983; 1985), neither the position (in the margin or embedded in the text) nor the nature of a heading (a statement as opposed to a question) had any effect on the retrieval of information. This seems to contradict the findings of Campbell Keagan Ltd (1990), where headings printed in the margin as white text in a black block made pages of text look easier to read, and made it simpler to locate specific sections of the text.

On occasions when it is important to indicate the sequence of headings, Lefrere et al. (1983) found that numbers were preferable to letters.

Poor designs which make it difficult to distinguish between headings seem to encourage skip reading (Campbell Keagan Ltd, 1990).

Swarts et al. (1980) demonstrated that inaccurate, incomplete or vague headings hindered readers who were looking for specific information in a text. This led Swarts et al. to conclude that effective headings are accurate, specific and focused on the reader's needs and goals.

4.3.3 Contents pages and indexes

Kempson and Moore (1994) maintain that contents pages make long documents more usable. Even though the initial impressions given by detailed contents pages are more off-putting than simpler ones, they ultimately make long documents easier to use (MIL Research Ltd, 1986a). Similarly, comprehensive and easy-to-use indexes increased the use of public documents (MIL Research Ltd, 1986b). According to FDS Ltd (1986), the poor indexing of UK Inland Revenue publications was one of the main reasons why solicitors and accountants preferred to use commercial publications.

4.4. Page design

The overall appearance of a document plays a critical part in its impact, acceptability and ease of use (Kempson and Moore, 1994). Readers' subjective assessments of the complexity of the content of information; their willingness to attempt particular tasks; and their impression of the value of the information is all influenced by the way in which information is visually presented (Reynolds,

1984). This section summarises research into the various aspects of page design. The presentation of type (typography), page layout, colour and graphics are all interacting aspects of page design (see Figure 4.1). Table 4.1 lists the main features of typography and page layout.

Table 4.1. Main features of typography and page layout

Typography	Page layout
■ Typefaces/fonts ■ Typestyle ■ Leading ■ Type size ■ Letter spacing ■ Word spacing ■ Text alignment ■ Hyphenation ■ Legibility	■ Page orientation ■ Columns ■ Headings ■ Margins and 'white space'

4.4.1 Legibility and typography

Legibility is one of the prime concerns of information designers. Reynolds (1984) presents guidelines on legibility and typography. She broadly defines legibility as 'those factors which may influence the ease, speed and accuracy with which information can be read.'

There is much research available concerning the legibility of text. The first studies were conducted in the early nineteenth century, although it was not until the beginning of the twentieth century that systematic investigations into the effects of design variables on reading performance were undertaken. Until relatively recently, most studies have been concerned with the design of continuous text which was traditionally typeset. These studies have identified a number of basic design factors which influence reading performance and have confirmed the value of many of the printer's traditional design practices (Reynolds, 1984). Today, however, alternative and cheaper methods of producing, printing and disseminating information — no longer exclusive to the design profession and printing industry — present additional reasons for investigating aspects of page design. With phototypesetting, for example, c h a r a c t e r   s p a c i n g   c a n   b e   v a r i e d   a t   w i l l; fonts can be enlarged, condensed, *italicized* or **changed in weight** with ease; and blocks of text can be manipulated in numerous ways. The effect on legibility and understanding of this revolution in publishing continues to be a subject of research.

Some of this research, however, is already obsolete. At the time of publication of Reynolds' guidelines in 1984 (which centred on the legibility of printed scientific and technical information), early versions of word-processing software were frequently used to provide camera-ready copy for offset-litho printing. Research into the legibility of dot-matrix copy, for example, has little significance in the current, new age of inkjet and laser printers. Other research (e.g. Tinker, 1963) whilst valid, is focused on detailed aspects of legibility such as character formation. The following is a discussion of research into features of typography and typesetting which are of particular relevance to the design of distance learning materials.

4.4.1.1 *Upper versus lower case letters*

It is generally accepted that text printed in lower case with few initial capital letters is easier to read than capital letters only (Kempson and Moore, 1994). This conclusion confirms the view of Spencer, et al. (1973) that lower case letters with their distinctive ascenders and descenders are generally more legible than their corresponding capitals (Reynolds, 1984).

In Wright's study (1979), lower case vertical typefaces with few capital letters were the easiest to read; the overuse of capital letters slowed readers down. In Wheildon's study (1984), fewer than one in ten adult volunteers found printed capital letters easier to read. Headlines in capitals were also found to be less legible than those set in lower case.

These studies all build upon the earlier conclusions of Tinker (1963) who found that all capital printing markedly reduced the speed of reading continuous text. Reductions of 13.9 per cent over a twenty minute reading period were recorded. This was thought to be due, in part, to words in lower case having more distinctive shapes than words in capitals and were therefore deemed easier to recognise. Reynolds (1988) also notes that text set entirely in capitals occupies 40 to 45 per cent more space than text in lower case of the same body size.

Under exceptional circumstances, however, where small type sizes approach the threshold of legibility, capital letters were found to be easier to discriminate than corresponding lower case letters (Tinker, 1963).

4.4.1.2 Typeface

The relative legibility of serif and sans-serif faces (e.g. Helvetica) has also been the subject of research with conflicting results. Serifs (e.g. Times Roman) have been thought to contribute to the individuality of letters and to the coherent formation of words, also helping to guide the eye along each line. Such claims have not been conclusively proved, however, and it appears that differences in legibility in favour of serifs may be due to familiarity rather than any intrinsic superiority (Reynolds, 1984).

Under laboratory conditions as set up by Suen and Komoda (1986), sans serif fonts were slightly more legible than serif fonts. There is also some evidence to suggest that sans-serif faces are more legible for children and poor vision readers (Reynolds, 1984).

4.4.1.3 Character size

For general readership, the ideal size for hand-held text is between 9 and 12 point (3mm to 4mm in height) where the optimum size is likely to be 10 or 11 point (Tinker, 1963). Speed of reading tends to be slower outside the range of 6 to 12 point. Though it may be true to say that type size has more effect on legibility than any other single typographic factor, readability is also determined by other critical factors such as content, length of line, and spacing between the lines (leading) (Wright, 1979; Reynolds, 1984).

According to Tinker (1963), type sizes larger than 14 point reduce the number of characters which can be perceived at each fixation. According to Vanderplas and Vanderplas (1980), however, the speed of reading of elderly people increases as the typesize increases, although there is no significant increase in reading speed over 14 point.

4.4.1.4 Type style, weight and underlining

There is overwhelming evidence to suggest that *italics* should not be used for large bodies of text. 96 per cent prefer Roman lower case (Tinker, 1963). This may be because the use of italics for more than a few words slows readers down (Wright, 1979). Wheildon (1984), however, claims that text in italics does not affect levels of comprehension.

Speed of reading tests have not revealed differences between **bold** and medium type, but 70 per cent of readers preferred the latter (Tinker, 1963). Others note that the use of bold type reduces comprehension and causes fatigue (Wright, 1979; Wheildon, 1984). This suggests that **bold type should only be used for emphasis** and not for continuous text (Reynolds, 1984).

A study by Hartley et al. (1980) found that both immediately, and in the long-term (a week later), recall was significantly better in children who had studied underlined text and that this result was not obtained at the expense of other items of information in the text.

There appears to be little evidence comparing the effectiveness of bold type with underlined text. Kempson and Moore (1984) note that most people believe intuitively that underlining words or phrases in a text helps in learning or absorbing text and that bold type is, in effect, the printer's equivalent.

4.4.1.5 Reversed type

Reynolds (1984) does not recommend the use of negative images (white type on a dark background) as the irradiation which occurs around the edges of bright images viewed against a dark background will tend to blur and thicken the type. Tinker (1963) demonstrates that in a normal reading situation black print on a white background is over ten per cent more efficient than white on black. Spencer et al. (1977) found paper opacity to be an important factor, noting that the 'show through' of print on subsequent pages which occurs with papers of low opacity — and exacerbated by type reversed out of blocks — can reduce legibility markedly.

4.4.1.6 Numerals

Numerals, like letters vary in legibility. Tests of modern and old style numerals showed that old style numerals which vary in height and alignment were more easily recognized at a distance that modern numerals which are all of the same height, but in normal reading situations the two kinds of numerals were read equally fast and with equal accuracy (Tinker, 1963). Arabic numerals (e.g. 3, 4, 5) are read significantly faster and more accurately than Roman numerals (e.g. iii, iv, v). The differences are so marked, particularly for numbers greater than ten, that there can be little justification for using Roman numerals in most cases (ibid.).

4.4.1.7 Text alignment and hyphenation

Wright (1979) suggests that people read faster when reading unjustified text than when reading text where the right-hand edge has been aligned vertically. Wheildon (1984), however, found the opposite to be true for adult readers of public documents. Gregory and Poulton (1970) concluded that less skilled readers were confused by the uneven spacing and hyphenation associated with justified setting. Other experiments have shown that there is little to choose between justified and unjustified composition in terms of legibility, reading speed or comprehension (Misanchuk, 1992; Hartley, 1994).

4.4.1.8 Line length

There is much evidence concerning the optimum number of characters per line of text. Some suggest that between 20 and 60 characters is the easiest to read and to understand (Wright, 1979; Wheildon, 1984; Frase et al., 1985). Spencer (1969) suggests that the optimum length of line is one which accommodates about ten to twelve words or 60 to 70 characters. Very short lines prevent maximum use of peripheral vision (Tinker 1963).

4.4.1.9 Line spacing (leading)

Space between lines (leading) is also seen to influence the ease of reading. According to Wright (1979), longer lines require more space between them for ease of reading.

4.4.1.10 Character and word spacing

Wright (1979) suggests that type with proportional spacing (such as this type) is easier to read than material with non-proportional spacing (where each letter or numeral takes up the same amount of space). Kerning (reducing the space between characters) leads to a reduction in the comprehension levels of adult readers (Wheildon, 1984), although students read close-spaced type more quickly (Moriarty and Scheiner, 1984). However, Spencer and Shaw (1971) suggest that small changes in letter spacing have no appreciable effect. They also concluded that small variations in word spacing are unlikely to affect legibility, but spacing should be such that it is sufficient to clearly separate adjacent words, yet not so great that the words cease to hold together as a line. Over-generous spacing can create vertical white 'rivers' of space on the page (Reynolds, 1984).

4.4.2 Semantic qualities of type

Choosing a typeface involves consideration of the impact it will have on the reader as well as consideration of its legibility. Editors of popular magazines, for example, often choose to set the replies to readers' letters in bold, sans serif type (**e.g. Helvetica Black**) to appear clear, concise and authoritative. The effect a typeface creates is often referred to as its 'semantic property', as opposed to the functional properties of size, boldness, contrast and aspects of form.

Semantic properties of type have been studied since the 1920s. In recent years, two notable projects have evaluated a number of typefaces on scales which measured their semantic properties (Bartram, 1982; Rowe, 1982). Typefaces were found to have perceptual qualities (such as 'hard-soft' or 'fast-slow') about which subjects generally agreed (Kempson and Moore, 1994). Furthermore, performance of simple classification tasks can be impaired if the meanings of words and the qualities of typeface are incongruous (Lewis and Walker, 1989). Bartram (1982) also noted that the semantic properties ascribed to typefaces by designers and non-designers were not always the same. Although there were similarities, there were also marked differences for most of the typefaces studied. From this it was recommended that designers should be aware that readers may not share their view of a typeface.

4.4.3 Page layout

Space and structure in text is considered here under the broad heading 'page layout', a term borrowed from the language of practising graphic designers which refers to the relationship and relative importance of text, images and space on any given page.

The various uses of type in the design of information are clearly important issues and are well researched. Hartley (1979), however, argues that there has been an imbalance in the consideration given to research into the 'molecular issues' of typography, compared with the 'molar issues' of space and structure of text.

Although he recognizes the contribution of Tinker (1963), he is critical of earlier researchers who 'ignored the higher-level organisational problems [of text] which in practice determine the decisions made at lower levels' (p.497). He observes that most of the knowledge gained from research into typography resulted from research which made no reference to the kind of text being printed, and with little of it being tested in the context of full pages of meaningful text.

The basis of Hartley's argument derives from observations of the working processes of typographic designers. He notes that of prime importance is how the document is to be used when it is printed. Consideration of this issue, he claims, leads to an appropriate choice of page size which is only then followed by 'secondary' decisions concerning type. He confirms that these secondary considerations are of considerable importance, but maintains that 'it is the use that is made of space on a page of known dimensions, rather than the type, that most affects the ease of comprehension and retrieval from printed text' (p.498).

Once a page size has been chosen appropriate to the needs of the reader, other decisions concerning the page layout of a document can be made (ibid.). In addition to the typographical issues discussed earlier, these include the vertical and horizontal spacing of text; the number of columns of text per page; the width of margins surrounding text blocks (often referred to as 'white space'); and the density of text in relation to graphics, illustrations or photographs.

4.4.3.1 Spacing of text

Hartley (1979; 1984; 1998) consistently argues that the spacing of text significantly affects comprehension. Here, spacing does not refer to the space between letters, words or lines as discussed earlier, but to the space that separates clauses, sentences, paragraphs, subsections and chapters from each other.

There is some research to confirm Hartley's view that spatial cues, such as a double amount of line spacing between paragraphs, are important aids to comprehension. Fisher (1976) argues that mature and experienced readers rely heavily on spatial cues to enhance their reading and search efficiency. Carpenter and Just (1977) demonstrate that the beginning of a line (and not the end) has a marked effect on eye-movement fixations and that text that starts in an irregular manner produces more regressive fixations than regularly spaced text.

Hartley (1979) extends his argument with reference to Haber (1978), maintaining that space helps readers to perceive redundancies in text, enabling them in turn to perceive effective from nominal stimuli, and thus focus on what is personally important. It is also space (between paragraphs, sections and chapters) that aids perception of the document structure as a whole, helping readers to understand it (ibid.).

4.4.3.2 *Single versus multiple column layouts*

Burnhill et al. (1976) suggest that a single-column layout is appropriate for the presentation of technical materials containing a large number of tables and diagrams. This confirmed an earlier study on the comprehension of scientific journals by Poulton (1959) which suggested that a larger typesize in a single column is preferable to smaller type in a double-column layout. Reynolds (1984) claims that a single column layout can be too wide for larger page sizes (such as A4) unless part of the page area is left unused.

4.4.3.3 *Margins and white space*

Page layouts which include 'white space' have been shown to have advantages. Some find it makes documents easier to follow (Nova Research Ltd, 1986).

According to Reynolds (1984), many book designers insist that text should only occupy 50 per cent of the page area on the grounds that the 'part-whole proportion illusion' encourages type to appear larger. There appears to be no evidence, however, to suggest that larger text occupying a greater proportion of the page area is any less satisfactory.

Some research suggests that margins help to reduce peripheral colour stimuli and prevent the eye 'from swinging off the page at the end of a return sweep' (ibid). Tinker (1963), however, argues that a wider margin gives no advantage and could only be adopted on aesthetic grounds. Reynolds (1984) adopts the practical approach of Spencer (1969), observing that wide margins provide space for making notes and allow the reader to hold the document without obscuring the text.

4.4.4 Graphics

Like many of the terms which are used within the printing and publishing industries, the term 'graphics' is used loosely. It usually refers to items on a page other than text and therefore includes photographs and illustrations. Illustration, however, is the focus of Part II, so the literature is considered separately and in more detail in Chapter 5.

It is worth noting here, however, that the term 'illustration' itself is a vague one. For the purpose of this research, an illustration is a picture or drawing which is intended to faithfully represent three-dimensional objects, or groups of objects, on a two-dimensional surface. In this sense, diagrams, which graphically represent data or concepts, are not illustrations (see Table 4.2). *The Concise Oxford Dictionary of Current English* (1976) defines a diagram as a 'drawing showing a general scheme or a graphic representation of the course or results of an action or process'.

4.4.4.1 *Tables*

Tables occupy the middle-ground between prose or blocks of text and graphics. They are usually composed of text, which are often numeric, but are nevertheless graphic representations of information.

Stubbs (1980) suggests that tables are one of the natural functions of written language. Tables have certainly played an important role in the history of the development of writing. Wright (1982) notes that inventories of various sorts form a large proportion of what remains of very early writings. Goody (1977) suggests that this is due to lists having no oral equivalent: i.e. it is unusual for people to recite lists of items in everyday conversation.

Wright (1981) notes that the ability to understand and interpret tabulated information requires special reading skills and that appropriate design of the information in tables can help readers who may only have a weak grasp of these skills. Reading tables involves understanding the logical principles on which the information has been organized; finding the required information in the table; and interpreting the information once it has been found (Wright, 1982).

According to Wright, specific design decisions have to be taken in a way that is both sensitive to the internal structure of the data being presented and to the needs of the readers who want to use the information. As such, she avoids universal guidelines, but makes some general observations based on research findings. She notes that eliminating redundancy can be a false economy: removing information from a table so that it requires less space 'often means that users have more problems trying to extract information from the table' (p.337). She also believes that designers of tables need to be able to use space to help readers perceive the 'functional groupings' within the material. Her research findings show, above all, that it is not sufficient for the information to be physically present on the page. 'Ease of use requires much more than this. In particular it requires the designer to be aware of how readers interact with printed materials' (ibid.).

Beach (1987) also reviews the principal typographic issues for presenting information in tables: i.e. the table structure, the alignment of rows and columns, the treatment of white space within tables, readability and the problem of breaking up large tables. Beach argues for the re-instatement of vertical rules (against current design trends) and the use of dotted leaders between columns to help the reader capture the content and meaning of the table.

4.4.4.2 Diagrams

Table 4.2 categorizes various types of diagrams.

Table 4.2. Examples of different types of diagrams

Quantitative	Non-quantitative
■ tables and spreadsheets	■ flow diagrams
■ line graphs	■ chronological charts
■ histograms and bar charts	■ relationship charts
■ area charts	■ maps
■ pie diagrams	
■ scatterplots	

Whereas tables have been used to categorize information since the early years of writing, the use of abstract, non-representational pictures to show numbers is a relatively recent invention, perhaps because of the diversity of skills required — the visual-artistic, empirical-statistical, and mathematical (Tufte, 1983). It was not until the late eighteenth century that statistical graphics (length and area to show quantity, time-series, scatterplots and multivariate displays) were invented — long after logarithms, Cartesian co-ordinates, the calculus, and the basics of probability theory (ibid.). William Playfair (1759-1832) developed or improved upon nearly all the fundamental graphic representations of data, seeking to replace conventional tables of numbers with the systematic visual representations of his 'linear arithmetic'.

According to Tufte (1983), modern data graphics can do much more than serve as a substitute for small statistical tables. At their best, he maintains, graphics are instruments for reasoning about quantitative information. He presents a theory which can lead to changes and improvements in the design of visual displays of quantitative information based on empirical measures of graphical performance. Although some of these suggested changes may be small, others are substantial. Writing in 1983, he estimates that each year somewhere between one and two trillion images of statistical graphics are printed, so improvements could impact on hundreds of billions of printed pages. He believes that excellence in statistical graphics consists of complex ideas communicated with clarity, precision and efficiency, and that graphical displays should:

- show the data;
- induce the viewer to think about the substance and not the method;
- avoid distorting what the data have to say;
- present many numbers in a small space;
- make large data sets coherent;
- encourage the eye to compare different pieces of data;
- reveal the data at several layers of detail, from a broad overview to the fine structure;
- serve a reasonably clear purpose: description, exploration, tabulation, or decoration; and
- be closely integrated with the statistical and verbal descriptions of a data set.

(Tufte, 1983: p.4)

The use of diagrams in a cross-cultural context has received considerable attention from authors concerned with communicating with communities who may not have been exposed to alternative forms of graphical representation. Diagrams are pivotal in participatory and rapid rural appraisal techniques. As Bradley (1995: p.7) notes:

'... knowledge [of the community] is clearly portrayed in the making of maps, seasonal diagrams, matrices, Venn diagrams and so on. Participation in this visual and public fashion reveals the value of indigenous knowledge. ... The fact that understanding and participation in mapping and diagramming are shared by the researchers and the villagers is of crucial importance. What has become obvious is that many more people share an understanding of diagrams than was thought previously.'

Diagrams are also widely used to enhance the information impact of instructional, learning and training materials at professional level. Cripwell (1989) notes, however, that little is known of non-picture visual literacy, the main reason being the lack of valid and reliable tests. Cripwell relates some of his experiences developing health learning materials in south-east Asia, as a consultant to the World Health Organization, and discusses a number of problems associated with the interpretation of outcome flowcharts, life cycle diagrams, pie charts, bar charts, instructional flowcharts, instructional diagrams and plotted graphs. He argues that barriers to an understanding of these non-representational forms are culturally determined and learners with little or no experience of their use may well find them incomprehensible. Despite this, he notes, learners can be trained to use them effectively.

4.4.4.3 Visual cues

Many instructional designers and researchers recommend the use of visual cues for directing students' attention to specific points in a text, believing that readers need assistance in locating the most important information (Kempson and Moore, 1994). The effects of such cues on recall were measured in a study of instructional texts by Beck (1984). This showed that recall was significantly greater when pictorial and textual cues were used together, but not when either type of cue was used alone.

4.4.5 Colour

The Department of Typography and Graphic Communication at Reading University, in association with Xerox, is currently reviewing the impact of colour on the comprehension of the printed page, given that access to a colour printing is dramatically increasing as the price of colour desk-top printers continue to fall and other forms of cost-effective printing are becoming available.

The first stage of the study has involved visits to around 20 different kinds of organization (such as government agencies, utilities, financial organizations, manufacturing and retail companies, consultancies of various kinds, research establishments, education, and the Health Service). Questions have centred on the extent to which organizations are using colour in internal office documents; how colour is used in different kinds of document; what are the perceived benefits of using colour; what disadvantages or difficulties have been encountered in using colour; and how organizations see their use of colour developing in the future.

The interest of the study lies not only in perceptions of the current technological constraints, but also in any other factors that organizations feel might be preventing them from making the best use of colour (such as a lack of design expertise).

The second stage of the Reading study will analyse a collection of documents produced by these and other organizations to find out more about the use of colour in relation to document content (how much colour is used, what colours are chosen, and what textual and graphic elements of the document colour is applied to). This will enable designers to make judgements about the effectiveness of current usage of colour in documents and to identify ways in which organizations might be helped to make more effective use of colour (Department of Typography and Graphic Communication, Reading University, 1999).

Chapter 5 continues the review of information design, focusing on research into representational illustration.

Chapter 5

Research into Illustration

5.1. Introduction

This chapter continues the review of literature into information design with a discussion of research into illustration which is the focus of the study reported in Part II.

The chapter begins by describing the role of illustrations in educational materials and the factors which affect their comprehension. It goes on to examine Goldsmith's analytical model leading to a discussion of particular aspects of illustration. It concludes with a discussion of the visual perception of engineering drawings and the cross-cultural implications of their use.

5.2. The role of illustrations in educational materials

Goldsmith (1984) cites Kennedy (1974) in the introduction to *Research into Illustration.*

> 'The aesthetics of pictures has been a rich and prominent topic for research.
> In contrast, the psychology of the informative uses of pictures lies scattered,
> its pieces needing to be brought together.'

Goldsmith responds to the challenge of bringing together the sources of research into educational illustration, by presenting the most comprehensive review of the subject until this date. She also presents an analytical model for evaluating the 'comprehensibility' of illustrations.

She begins her review with a discussion of whether, in any given context, illustrations should be used at all, a subject which has been the focus of research in its own right. Goldsmith notes, however, that this is a 'circular problem, because from all the relevant studies only one general conclusion can be drawn: it all depends.' (p.11)

She expands on this, however, by suggesting that the most important factors which affect the decision to use illustrations are *educational objectives* and *student characteristics*. These conclusions are drawn from several sources, notably Dwyer (1972). Dwyer, himself, tables a number of variables within these two categories (Table 5.1):

Table 5.1. Factors affecting the decision to use illustrations

Educational objectives	Student characteristics
■ factual information ■ visual identification ■ terminology ■ comprehension ■ total understanding	■ age ■ mental ability ■ learning style and attitude ■ cultural factors ■ interest and motivation to learn ■ creativity ■ verbal and conceptual ability ■ perception ■ prior experience and knowledge ■ grade level.

Source: Dwyer, 1972

5.2.1 Achieving educational objectives with illustrations

The first question Goldsmith believes it is necessary to consider when faced with a choice of using an illustration to achieve any given educational objective, is whether the *content* of the illustration is strongly visual. She cites Dwyer's studies where, for example, 'the drawing of the heart was clearly the most economical way of demonstrating the position of its component parts' (p.77). She acknowledges, however, that 'the names and functions of those parts were, in some cases, more easily dealt with verbally' (ibid.). Tennyson (1978: p.297) offers a general guideline:

' ... drawings can have a significant effect on learning concepts and rules when they serve as images for encoding content for later use as well as initial learning. As a design strategy, therefore, a visual should be structured to represent the thesis of a paragraph or its salient ideas.'

Goldsmith's review of research includes many examples of illustrations used to support children's learning, as well as studies with a cross-cultural focus. In the latter case, she concludes that there is 'little doubt that in communicating in print with people who cannot read, pictures are essential' (p.78), a conclusion commonly supported by many authors concerned with international development and communication at village-level, including Fuglesang (1982) and Linney (1995) whose writings are reviewed, among others, by Bradley (1995).

What is not included in Goldsmith's discussion of student characteristics is the extent to which illustrations are important to students who are literate and educated, but whose cultural and educational background differ from those of the illustrator. Nevertheless, Tennyson's guideline seems a reasonable one to adopt in circumstances where illustrations are deemed essential. Where pictures are not believed to be strictly necessary, their use may be determined by the developmental level of the student (Goldsmith, 1984).

Whilst the imposition of imagery perceived to be irrelevant may affect the motivation of students, Goldsmith notes, the decision whether to use non-essential illustrations is less critical than for other media 'since students are always free to ignore the illustrations' (ibid., p.79).

5.2.2 Factors affecting the comprehension of illustrations

Illustrations in educational materials can perform many functions which range from the provision of technical information (where total comprehension of the illustration is essential) to complementing prose-based information and stimulating attention (where total comprehension may not be necessary).

Many distance learning packages make use of illustrations in a variety of ways. Brody (1981) reviews research which relates to instructional textbooks, by which the author means textbooks that are designed and used primarily for the purpose of direct instruction in a specific academic discipline or subject and for a specific audience. The review is worth noting here as this definition can be directly applied to distance learning as defined in Chapter 3. Brody suggests that there are major shortcomings in most published research which has tended to focus on simple illustrations such as line drawings, that are not representative of those found in instructional texts. Brody argues for a more functional approach to research, concentrating on the precise mechanisms by which illustrations aid learning.

Duchastel (1980) also argues that research into illustration in educational and instructional texts is 'confused' and that little can be learned from the research. He suggests that where research has tried to find out if illustrations can enhance learning, little recognition has been made of the fact that the term 'illustration' is a generic one covering a wide range of formats such as photographs, schematic drawings, diagrams and maps. Similarly, little of the research has taken account of the purpose of including illustrations in a text, to either interest or motivate the reader, to help explain a point made in the prose, or to enhance long-term recall of the prose.

Duchastel notes that whilst a few studies have shown that illustrations can aid comprehension, a large number have not. This situation arises, he believes, because the research does not taken account of the fact that some materials do not need illustrations to be understood. He concludes by arguing for a shift in the focus for pictorial research, believing that more attention needs to be given to the functional approach (what a picture does in a particular context) rather than the 'morphological approach' where the prime concern is what a picture looks like (Kempson and Moore, 1994).

In the second part of her review, Goldsmith (1984) adopts a functional approach. Her analytical model provides a useful framework for discussion of the research into specific aspects of illustration.

5.3. Goldsmith's analytical model

The purpose of a model for the analysis of illustrations is to ensure that, where pictures are used in an educational context, they will be used to their best effect. Without such a model, designers of educational materials are left to assume that there is an ideal illustration which can either be included or left out according to the various demands of context. In practice, of course, there is no such thing as 'every illustration produced is different in an infinite number of ways from every other illustration' (Goldsmith, 1984: p.123).

5.3.1 Response levels

Goldsmith's initial suggestion is that comprehension involves three different levels of response:

- a response to graphic signals as an image or set of images;

- a response to an image in terms of the meanings the artist intended to set down; and

- a response to the artist's meanings in terms of all the previous experience and present judgement of the viewer.

She proposes that the study and analysis of illustration should be undertaken at these three levels. Adopting the terminology of Morris (1938) she describes the first level as *syntactic* which does not presuppose any recognition of images; the second *semantic* which refers to the literal identification of an image such as might be provided by a dictionary definition; and the third *pragmatic* which implies interpretation by a viewer, the stage at which the comprehension of a picture may depend on developmental, cultural or similar factors.

Goldsmith emphasizes that these levels are often interdependent in practice, and that in any case, consideration of the higher levels presupposes the existence of those below.

5.3.2 Visual factors

Goldsmith also suggests that certain visual factors should be considered in a way that is related to these three levels. These factors are:

Unity — an area of a picture (or an object) which might be recognised as having a separate identity, even if the identity is not known.

Location — the spatial relationship between objects within a picture.

Emphasis — the hierarchical relationship between objects within a picture (i.e. their levels of importance).

Text parallels — the relationship between a picture and its supporting text.

Goldsmith's model is constructed on the interaction of these four factors and the three levels of response. Table 5.2 below presents an adaptation of her matrix.

Table 5.2. Goldsmith's matrix for the analysis of illustrations

	SYNTACTIC (image recognition)	SEMANTIC (image identification)	PRAGMATIC (viewer interpretation)
UNITY (area of a picture/object with own identity)	**1.** Recognition of the bounds of an area of a picture or an object	**2.** Identification of an area of a picture or an object	**3** The role of experience and context in the interpretation of an area of an image or an object
LOCATION (spatial relationship between areas of a picture/objects)	**4** Basic pictorial depth perception	**5** The contribution of object identification to the perception of pictorial depth	**6** Experimental factors in pictorial depth perception
EMPHASIS (hierarchical relationship between objects within picture)	**7** The attraction and direction of attention, independent of meaning	**8** Descriptive objects having widespread attraction and direction value	**9** The influence of extra-pictorial factors on scanning behaviour
TEXT PARALLELS (relationship between picture and its supporting text)	**10** Relationship between illustration and supporting text	**11** The naming or description of an illustration	**12** The conceptual relationship between text and illustration

Source: After Goldsmith, 1984, p.126

5.4. Aspects of illustration

The following discussion of specific aspects of illustration draws on elements of Goldsmith's matrix. Much of the research reviewed by Goldsmith relates to child development, but there are also significant findings concerning education and culture.

5.4.1 The bounds of a single image

The first aspect of illustration presented in the matrix is the most basic level of pictorial perception: discrimination of the bounds of an image. Goldsmith reviews the research by Deregowski (1968) in Zambia, and Deregowski, Muldrow and Muldrow (1972) in Ethiopia who reported no evidence of difficulty at what they call the 'detection' level of pictorial perception. This finding was corroborated by Kennedy and Ross (1975) in New Guinea.

The research at this simple level, as well as being focussed on the perceptual abilities of populations with suspected low-levels of visual literacy, has also focussed on the perceptual abilities of children, for example Ghent (1956).

Goldsmith concludes that the ability to distinguish the bounds of an image is universally very high given an acceptable level of visual literacy, and that it may be reasonably assumed that for the educated, professional adult learner, any failure to understand a picture is unlikely to occur at this level.

5.4.2 Image recognition

As with the research into the recognition of the bounds of a single image, research into image recognition has also tended to focus on populations with suspected low-levels of visual literacy, and not with educated populations. Many studies, for example Travers (1969), Fussell and Haaland (1978), and Cook (1980) show detailed line drawings to be the most readily recognisable form of illustrative depiction in general. Most problems with image recognition have been observed in the studies of young children and people from cultures who have not come into contact with many pictures, especially adults over forty years old. Figure 5.1 (taken from the study by Holmes (1963) of 1544 adolescents and adults having undergone between two and eight years' formal education in Kenya) lists some of the 'correct' and 'incorrect' interpretations of the pictures illustrated.

In general, however, recognition of familiar objects is universally high, although 'some doubt has been expressed regarding the depiction of people or objects truncated by the picture frame, in illustrations intended for use in a cross-cultural context, or with young children' (Goldsmith, 1984, p165).

Figure 5.1. **Results from *A Study of Understanding of Visual Symbols in Kenya***

Correct answers Fly; Teste fly **Incorrect answers** Don't know; mosquito; locust; butterfly; grasshopper; spider; lice. **Percentage correct: 71.2**	**Correct answers** Flies on faeces; flies **Incorrect answers** Birds; dead body; don't know; sun; vultures; a hill; a lake; a duck; a cave; white ants; hippo; Mount Kenya (many); rain. **Percentage correct: 12.1**
Correct answers Map; Map of Kenya (extended meaning) **Incorrect answers** Don't know; water; East Africa; skin; cloth; shirt; map of world; a pit; a skin being dried; a hill. **Percentage correct: 20**	**Correct answers** Eye; sight **Incorrect answers** Don't know; mosquito; hat; feeding bottle; fly; head; fish; larva on a leaf; a stone; worm on a leaf; the sun; germs; snail; pupa of fly; a bird; maggot; crocodile. **Percentage correct: 82.4**

Source: Holmes, 1963

5.4.3 The role of experience and context in recognition

Research into this area of illustration takes into account how much of a bearing characteristics of the individual viewer will have on the recognition of an image, for example: age, ability, experience, culture and background. Relevant aspects are grouped by Goldsmith (1984) under the headings:

- **Familiarity of the depicted object** — where studies have focussed on the ability to categorise unfamiliar objects (Holmes, 1963; Deregowski, 1968; Shaw, 1969; and Kennedy and Ross, 1975).

- **Specificity of identification** — where the ability of the viewer to discriminate finely can be a disadvantage, when generality is the aim (Shaw, 1969). To illustrate this point, Jenkins (1978) tells an anecdote about a primary school teacher from rural Yorkshire:

  'This is a hilly region of England where there is a lot of sheep farming. She drew a picture of a sheep on the blackboard and asked the children what it was. She was puzzled at the silence. After a while she discovered that the children were puzzling over its features and trying to work out what kind of sheep it was. Sheep were so much part of their lives that they could not recognize a generalized sheep.' (p.32)

- **The use of context** — which reduces the possibilities of interpretation (Hochberg; 1972).

- **Understanding of implied movement** — where studies have demonstrated that a number of devices commonly used by artists to depict movement show acceptance of posture as an indicator (e.g. a running man), but little understanding of more arbitrary conventions such as speed lines and blurs (Friedman and Stevenson, 1975; Saiet, 1979). (See Figure 5.2.)

81

Figure 5.2. Implied motion

Source: Duncan, Gourlay and Hudson, 1973

5.4.4 Basic pictorial depth perception

Basic pictorial depth perception is seen as either innate and universal (e.g. Gibson, 1950; Hagen and Jones, 1978; Greenberg, 1978), or as a learned ability (e.g. Hudson, 1960). There is much evidence to suggest that accurate perspective drawings, particularly those incorporating grids, are compelling in their effect on Western adults (e.g. Hayes and King, 1967) but this does not necessarily mean that Westerners have always been susceptible to these illusions.

Goldsmith (1984) believes that 'we may for all practical purposes assume that some fundamental responses to depth in some pictures is present at a very early stage in development'. Development in this case refers to the increasing ability to understand pictures among people whose culture does not commonly have access to pictorial materials, as well as to children generally.

5.4.5 Image identification and the perception of pictorial depth

The way in which identification of an image contributes to the perception of pictorial depth are illustrated by five studies discussed by Goldsmith (1984) covering two different applications of this factor. There is the *familiar size* of isolated objects, such as birds and elephants which occupy multiplane space (e.g. Hudson, 1960; Hagen and Glick, 1977); and the recognition of a context such as sea or grass which receded continuously (Rock, Shallo and Schwartz, 1978).

The perception of pictorial depth by the familiar size of separate objects appears to be very weak when used without the support of other visual depth cues, although ignoring the known size of objects when constructing a picture, Goldsmith (1984) suggests, 'may not be wise'. It is possible that the perception of depth by familiar size would be stronger for populations whose cultural traditions represent size according to the importance of the object, or use the picture plane to determine proximity, but there appears to be no evidence to either confirm or contradict this (ibid.).

Rock, Shallo and Schwartz (1978) consider identification of the pictorial elements, in particular those which occupy continuous space, to be necessary for the perception of depth, even to the extent of dispensing with traditional pictorial cues. Although they make a convincing argument for identification being in some cases a significant factor, others, especially Goldsmith (1984), do not agree that it is essential to such perception except in the absence of most other cues.

5.4.6 The effect of experience on pictorial depth perception

The literature reveals that viewers' knowledge of 'the way things are in the real world' affects their perception of pictorial depth (Goldsmith, 1984: p.240). Mundy-Castle (1966) comments on the influence on meaning by referring to the response of a girl of seven to one of Hudson's test pictures: 'The goat can't see the man because if it could it would run away and not stand there.' (p.297)

Some experiments have demonstrated that it is necessary to see depth in a picture before an image can be identified. This occurred in Shaw's study (1969) where a zebra crossing was only named correctly by 7 per cent of the subjects until people were depicted using it when recognition increased to 18 per cent. Earlier incorrect responses of 'flag' and 'house' could indicate problems with the understanding of perspective which, according to Dawson (1967a and 1967b) exist in some cultures and sub-cultures. Goldsmith (1984) concludes that the 'evidence of cultural differences in perception of pictorial depth is overwhelming … and there is little doubt that care needs to be taken in the presentation of materials for other cultures.' (p.244)

Some authors (e.g. Linney, 1985) question whether preparation of materials by outsiders is appropriate and have concentrated on helping communities to create their own visual materials based on local pictorial conventions. This is the practical application of the philosophies of Freire (1974), and later Fuglesang (1982) who believe that the preparation of visual materials for other cultures has been used in the West as a means of suppressing the poor.

5.4.7   Attraction and direction of attention independent of meaning

The effects of a lack of emphasis in a picture are well illustrated in Figure 5.3 also taken from the study by Holmes (1963). The attempt to provide a context in this case reduced the percentage of correct responses (boy defecating). Wrong answers include 'house', 'house and flowers', 'person at home', 'planting flowers', 'child playing in garden', and 'clean house'. Often context is essential, however, and it becomes important to manipulate the levels of emphasis when the message must be transmitted accurately as, for example, in first aid instruction (Goldsmith, 1984).

Figure 5.3. Boy defecating

Source: Holmes, 1963

There is much agreement among researchers concerning effective devices for attracting, holding and directing attention, including the following factors: colour, tonal contrast, position, size, and isolation which are described below. They appear to be of prime importance when the communication potential of a picture (or series of pictures) is being considered, whoever the intended viewers may be (Goldsmith, 1984). While each of these factors has an attraction value, however, they can also *distract* attention (Rutherford et al., 1979; Reid and Miller; 1980).

- **Colour and tonal contrast.** It appears from the literature that it is not colour in itself which is important: it is the contrast it provides with surrounding areas. Brandt (1945) comments that if large areas of a display were in colour, then black and white would prove to be the focus of attraction. Kelly (1965) provides a list of twenty-two maximum contrast colours which could be helpful in cases where there is an opportunity to use a few strong colours. Smith and Watkins (1972) found that a single additional colour was effective in line drawings.

- **Position.** Brandt (1945) claims that 'of all the physical variables studied … position is one of the strongest physical determiners of attention' (p.47), and points out in his experiment with the attraction value of colour, that regardless of the colour or the character of the design, viewers spent more time looking at areas on the left and top halves of the page than on the right and bottom halves.

- **Size.** The part of the eye which sees most clearly (the fovea) is capable of focussing on only a small area at a time, so to attract attention it is sometimes necessary to design material which contains elements discernible by peripheral vision (Goldsmith, 1984). The reference of Brandt (1945) to size as an attractor is less concerned with initial attraction than with sustained attention. He found that increasing the size of a picture resulted in a greater amount of time being devoted to it, but only in proportion to its linear increase: that is an area four times the size held the interest of the viewer for twice the length of time.

- **Isolation.** This is a form of emphasis traditionally exploited by typographers and is referred to in the previous chapter as 'white space'. According to Goldsmith (1984), it seems to have been neglected by researchers in pictorial perception, except for Brandt's experiments with layouts which varied in the amount of white space surrounding each picture. He found the optimum amount of white space for promoting sustained attention was 25 per cent of the total display area, but he did not measure the effect of isolation on the attraction of attention.

Little work seems to have been done on the relative strengths of the above factors, although Brandt (1945) claims that *position* is the strongest of all the variables he tested.

5.4.8   The attraction and direction value of descriptive images

By far the most universal descriptive form of attraction is the human figure: in particular the face, and more precisely still, the eyes and mouth (Goldsmith, 1984). If the figure is placed so that features are clearly visible, it can perform the function not only of attraction but of direction of attention since there is a reliable tendency for viewers to follow the depicted direction of the gaze (ibid.).

5.4.9   The influence of extra-pictorial factors

There is some suggestion that certain cultures find the particular dimensions of a picture to be more important than others, but most of the research in this area has focussed on the scanning patterns of children. Some of the findings reveal that until around the age of twelve or thirteen, younger children are unable to ignore irrelevant information in pictures and rarely complete the search of complex pictures.

5.4.10   Spatial relationships between text and illustrations

The ways in which the position of text with pictures affects comprehension has been the subject of some studies. The extensive study of text/illustration relationships by Smith and Watkins (1972) was inconclusive, although they still maintained that 'where illustrations are important for comprehension, the layout of both text and illustrations is a critical factor.' (p.20)

Goldsmith (1984) believes that it is 'probably true' that the arrangement of pictures with text 'will have an effect on perception and comprehension, but that … any possible effects on learning would be too subtle to measure' (p.328). Whalley and Flemming (1975) concluded that 'the use of a predictable relationship between the diagram and the piece of text relevant to it would result in the reader achieving a greater feeling of understanding than if the text/diagram relationship was unpredictable' (p.121). Goldsmith (1984) suggests that 'the question of whether the text should be continuous or divided into short passages by illustrations has to be dictated by the content of the instructional material' (p.328).

Beyond the adoption of a consistent method of presentation when relating text to illustrations, natural scanning habits can be exploited to facilitate eye movements (Goldsmith, 1984). Brandt (1945) and Buswell (1935) demonstrate with fixation records that in a document containing both text and pictures, the pictures will be the first to attract attention. The eye moves horizontally to the right or vertically downwards, unless there are other forms of emphasis to compensate for this tendency.

5.4.11 The conceptual relationship between meaning and pictures

Of the specific aspects of illustration described in this section, the conceptual relationship between meaning and illustration is one of the most complex, given that the focus here is not solely on identification, depth, or emphasis, but on all of these aspects at once, together with the past experience each viewer brings to the interpretation of pictures.

Perhaps the main consideration in respect of the relationship between text and a picture is whether it is intended that one should replicate the other; and if not, then the proportion of the total communication that each is expected to contribute. In many cases in educational illustration, it is intended that the text and the picture should convey as nearly as possible the same message to the viewer. Text varies in the extent to which it lends itself to a pictorial form of expression. While the main idea of a paragraph might be conveyed by a competent illustrator, the depiction of a simple sentence can sometimes cause problems.

An example of this can be found in Bratt (1978) who approached the problem of designing pictorial labels for medicine bottles. In New York during the early 1970s he noticed that an estimated 80 to 85 per cent of the population made mistakes in following prescriptions. Bratt believed this reflected the nature of the population of 'ghetto' areas who neither spoke nor understood English adequately. Labels suitable for both eye ointment and eyedrops were developed and tested on a hundred literates and a hundred illiterates (Figure 5.4).

Figure 5.4. Third versions of Bratt's pictorial designs for medicine labels

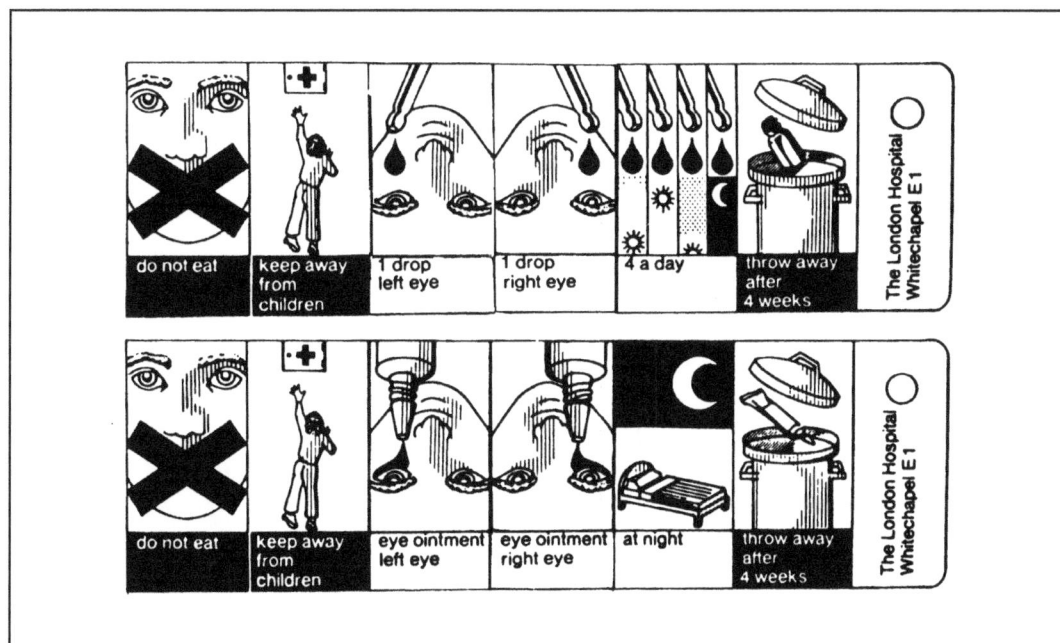

Source: Bratt, 1978

'The only instruction which it was not found possible to illustrate in a way comprehensible to the majority of illiterates was *Throw away after 4 weeks*. The rest of the images incorporated in the final design were understood by at least 65 per cent of illiterates, the best being achieved by the cautions *Do not eat* and *Keep away from children*.' (p.35)

In isolated cases, the conceptual use of illustrations can be counter-productive. Attempts by Fussel and Haaland (1978: p.27) to make villagers in Nepal draw their own pictures to represent messages was not a success:

'It was not only that the villagers did not know how to draw, or what to draw, although of course this was a problem as many of them had not handled drawing materials before. The very idea of drawing a picture to convey a message struck them as strange. One villager was handed drawing materials and asked "If there was something dangerous near your village, what could you put near it to warn people away?". "A big stone wall" replied the villager, putting the drawing materials to one side.'

Most cross-cultural studies, however, have shown that a basic understanding of pictures exists in remote cultures even if this is only a recognition that an image can be intended to represent a three-dimensional object. Most surveys, however, report misunderstandings at higher levels and are misunderstandings of interpretation rather than identification (Goldsmith, 1984).

Problems arise in the presentation of arbitrary symbols and the application of colours; and when attempting to convey extended or figurative meanings. Not only do images and colours symbolize different things to people from different cultures, but the connotations of certain types of dress or environment may not be the same for artist and viewer. Furthermore, the acceptability of a depicted event is an important consideration. If offence is given, or distress caused, there will be no communication at all (ibid.).

Two cases reported by Garland (1982) demonstrate problems with the acceptability of images. The first version of the picture shown in Figure 5.5 was rejected because the exposure of legs when squatting was not culturally acceptable to subjects. Bare legs were also the cause of an objection raised in the case of the first version shown in Figure 5.6. The second version still showed too much leg, and further modifications had to be carried out. In addition, the women were claimed to be too Western-looking.

Figure 5.5. Defecating

Source: Garland, 1982

Figure 5.6. Nurse fitting a contraceptive diaphragm

Source: Garland, 1982

This point is particularly relevant to this research. Distance learning materials intended for a global audience cannot be easily changed or 'tailored' to conform to local sensibilities. Although educated learners may be aware of the symbolic differences of artistic conventions employed in materials originating from other regions of the world, and be generous in their interpretation of these, they could still cause offence.

5.5. Visual perception of engineering drawings

Development work is multi-disciplinary by nature, so many professionals choosing to undertake a distance learning programme in the planning, provision, or management of infrastructure are non-technologists, and may have received little or no training in the interpretation of engineering drawings and technical illustrations. Anecdotal accounts also suggest that engineers themselves may not necessarily be highly practised in these skills (Ince 1997; Reed 1997). Yet the interpretation of such drawings is essential to understanding the technical options available to a development project and for communicating the likely impact a particular choice will have on a community.

Davies (1973) raises a number of interesting and important issues concerning the visual perception of engineering drawings. These are considered here as they directly relate to the focus of the research into appropriate methods of projecting three-dimensional objects in two-dimensions reported in Part II.

Davies (1973) describes engineering drawing as 'a language which expresses itself through the medium of lines instead of words' (p.22). He recognizes that 'this language has been considered far superior to any other system of communication and that information, particularly technical information, transmitted in pictorial form is universally understood' (ibid.). He also recognizes that the level of spatial ability necessary to visualize a three-dimensional object drawn on a plane surface varies between groups of students.

If we accept that some variation exists in levels of spatial perception in our own culture it follows that the differences will be even greater between cultures where alternative codes are employed for defining pictorial space (ibid.). Davies (1973) notes that the problem is acute for students seeking 'technological education' in the West or even within their own educational system if that system is based on a Western model. He cites a number of the studies reviewed by Goldsmith and discussed in the previous sections, and is forceful in his assessment of the results which 'indicate that there are persistent and significant differences in the way pictorial information is interpreted by people of different cultures and that this perception calls for some form of learning.' (ibid.).

Segall et al.(1966) reviewing a number of experiments carried out to validate this learning theory commented that the visual perception of objects distributed in space comes to us with such vivid directness and clarity that it is hard to imagine that vision is affected by learning.

Hudson (1960) concluded that formal education did not play a decisive role in the growth of pictorial depth perception which he associated more with informal parental instruction and exposure to pictures. Hudson's methods and the validity of his results have since been questioned by several researchers (Goldsmith, 1984). Davies (1973) concludes that it is always pertinent to review the results and conclusions reached by psychologists studying the nature of visual perception in various continents of the developing world to ascertain whether we can improve our methods of transmitting information pictorially.

In engineering drawing, Davies (1973) notes, the perception of pictorial information can be considered from two aspects: the spatial perception of a draughtsman to produce suitable drawings of an object from a given specification, and that required by the engineer to manufacture the component from the drawings. These two processes require different forms of perception. Whilst the draughtsman tries to show a three-dimensional object on a two-dimensional plane surface, the engineer must create a three-dimensional object by working from the two-dimensional representation of the object.

The emphasis on developing visualization skills for the development professional (whether or not he or she has an engineering background) lies in interpretation of drawings, rather than on their production, since draughting is a specialist skill and one that, in any case, can now be readily produced from a computer-aided design system.

Nevertheless, the questions concerning the most effective ways of representing information in pictorial form remain. Davies (1973) asks:

'Should we use ... perspective projection, or oblique projection, or should we use orthographic projection. ... The easiest way of showing all the details of an object on paper using two-dimensional plane surfaces is to use orthographic projection, since characteristics of the object can be shown which cannot be seen from a single viewpoint. But is this the best way? Orthographic projection is, understandably, the easiest way for a draughtsman to relate all the features of a three-dimensional object on paper, but for the engineer trying to interpret the object, a form of pictorial projection would be better.'

(Davies, 1973: p.23)

Little use is made in engineering drawing of the pictorial depth cues, (such as familiarity, familiar size, overlap, emphasis, isolation, colour, tonal contrast and context discussed above) which help most people associate pictures with the physical world. Since the 1970s many successful attempts have been made to produce suitable technical illustrations for development which have a broad appeal and reach out to non-engineers. Figure 5.7 is an example of such an illustration designed for use at field level. Questions still remain however, concerning the relative merits of different types of projection at professional level. These questions take on a greater significance when technical illustrations need to 'stand alone', supported by text, but not by the verbal explanations of a tutor, such as illustrations for distance learning.

Part II of this thesis reports the attempts to seek answers to some of the questions raised above.

Figure 5.7. Lining a well

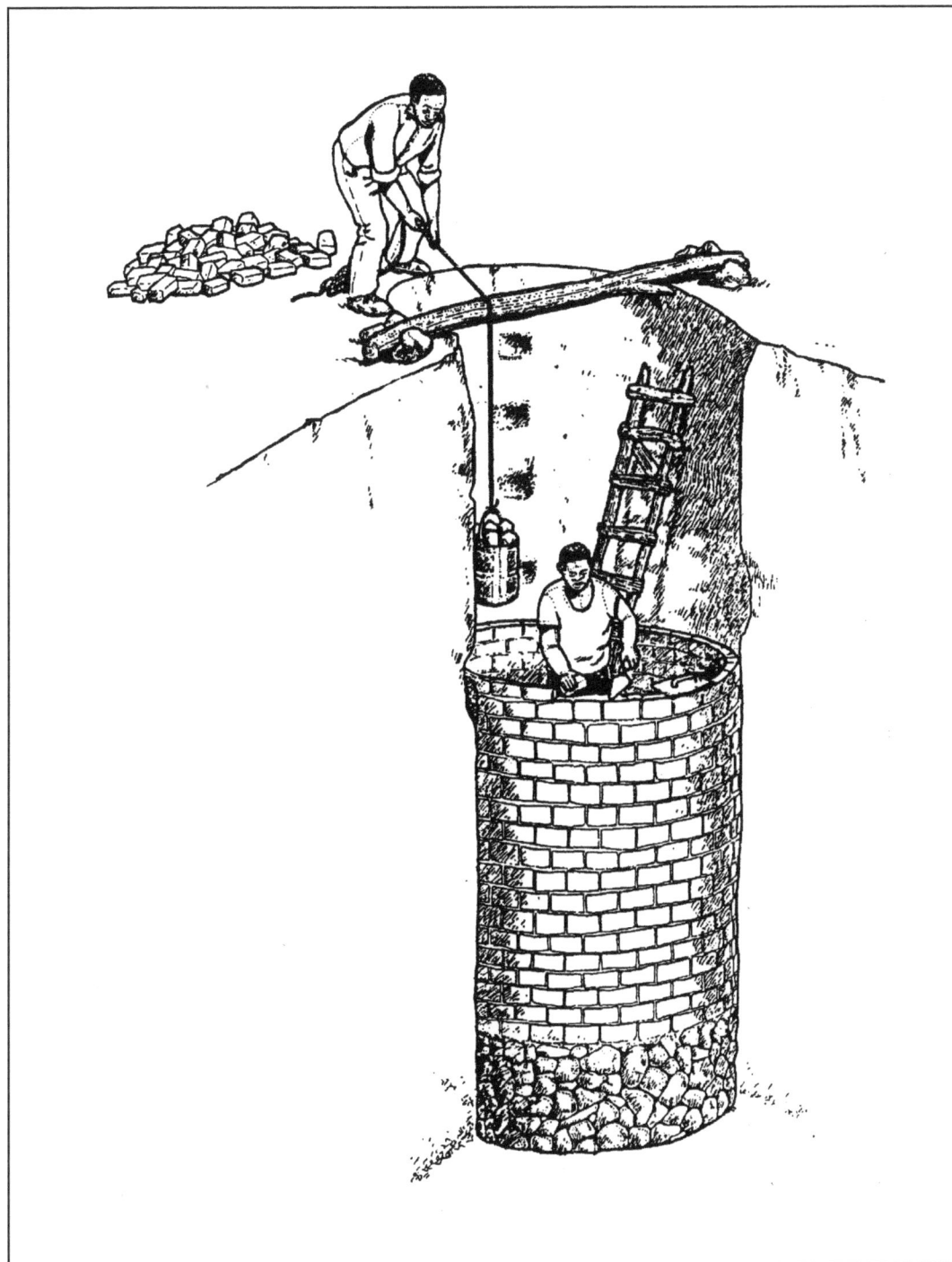

Source: Morgan, 1990

PART II

Chapter 6

Hypotheses

6.1. Introduction

Part I of this thesis examined, and made connections between, literature concerned with learning and education; international development and distance learning; information design for self-instruction; and research into illustration. It provides the basis for Part II of the thesis.

Section 6.2 of this chapter raises questions about the use of projection systems for illustrations designed to support distance learning in a cross-cultural context. These have arisen as a consequence of the earlier discussions presented in Part I. Part II sets out to address these questions by testing a series of hypotheses, analysing the data produced from these tests, and discussing the implications of the results.

Section 6.3 presents a list of variables which relate to the hypotheses. Section 6.4 presents the research hypotheses themselves, and Section 6.5 describes the projection systems under study. Chapter 7 describes and explains the methodology used for testing the hypotheses. Chapter 8 reports the results of the tests and Chapter 9 presents the analyses and discussion of the results. Conclusions are drawn in Chapter 10.

6.2. Questions

The literature review of research into illustration revealed that an analysis of the precise 'mechanisms' by which illustrations assist comprehension is required before recommendations can be made about the design, or choice, of illustrations in any given educational context.

One such mechanism is the pictorial representation of three-dimensional space. Illustrations which visually describe the three-dimensional nature of objects and infrastructure can reduce and even eliminate the need for written explanations. It is this principle which gave rise to the rapid development of engineering drawing as the engineer's primary communication tool during the Western Industrial Revolution of the nineteenth century.

A number of engineering drawing systems have since evolved. These are sets of visual codes and rules which enable the draughtsman and viewer to share the same vision of a proposed object or structure. Only with a thorough understanding of the rules and codes used to produce the drawings, however, will the viewer be able to understand and make good use of them.

It was noted in the last chapter that many professionals choosing to undertake a distance learning programme in the planning, provision, or management of infrastructure are non-technologists and, as such, may have received little or no training in de-coding engineering drawings and technical illustrations. However, many text books and other publications, typical of those which might support distance learning programmes in infrastructure development, use engineering drawing projection systems as the basis for the illustrative content. Orthographic projections, third angle projections, isometric projections, perspective views and cross-sections are all commonly used.

This raises the following questions:

Q.1. Which particular projection system (or systems) best supports adult learning in a cross-cultural context?

Q.2. Do some groups of adult learners find it easier to understand the pictorial conventions of engineering drawing systems than other groups? If so, can this be attributed to socio-cultural, academic or other variables (such as those listed in Section 6.3)?

6.3. Variables

1.   Age

2.   Artistic background

3.   Country of birth

4.   Country of childhood

5.   Country of education

6.   Country of permanent residence

7.   Course of study

8.   Economic region of permanent residence

9.   Educational level

10.   English as first language

11.   Ethnic origin

12.   Formal training in engineering drawing / technical drawing

13.   Gender

14.   Handedness

15.   Nationality

16.   Professional status

17.   Religious background

18.   Work experience

Answers to these questions would have important implications for the ways in which illustrations for distance learning materials are produced. The questions are easy ones to ask, but they demand comprehensive answers. Although the scope of this research does not allow for a full study of all projection systems and all adult learning groups, it is hoped that by testing the following hypotheses and analysing and discussing the results, a significant contribution to the answers can be made.

6.4. Hypotheses

Hypothesis 1 (H1) relates to the first question. Hypotheses 2 and 3 (H2 and H3) focus on the ability of groups of adult learners, defined by a range of variables (presented in Section 6.3) to understand projection systems used in engineering drawings.

H1. **Isometric projections of three-dimensional space are easier to understand than third-angle projections.**

H2. **The ability of adult learners to understand the pictorial conventions of third-angle projections and isometric projections is significantly affected by one or more of the variables listed in Section 6.3.**

H3. **The relative importance of linear perspective as a means of understanding pictorial space is significantly affected by one or more of the variables listed in Section 6.3.**

6.5. Descriptions of the projection systems studied

6.5.1 Third-angle projection

The *orthographic projection* is the most common type of projection in engineering. The lines of sight from the eye to the object are parallel and perpendicular to the plane of projection. A *third-angle projection* comprises three orthographic projections arranged so that dimensions can be transferred from one view to another.

6.5.2 Isometric projection

Axonometric projection is a means of adding pictorial depth to orthographic projections. Isometric projection is a type of axonometric projection where the angle of inclination to all three planes are equal. The three main axes are projected on a drawing sheet so that they are 120° to each other. All three dimensions, length, width and height are projected with the same scale. Parallel lines on the actual object are projected parallel on the view.

6.5.3 Linear perspective

The term *perspective* is often used in a wide sense and refers to any graphic method by which an impression of three-dimensional space is represented on a two-dimensional surface. Here, perspective refers specifically to a particular drawing procedure governed by the rules of *linear perspective* devised during the Renaissance period of Western art of the sixteenth century, and which are based on the observation that parallel lines of objects which recede to the distance appear to converge at a single point.

Figure 6.1.   Example representations of a rectangular block using the three types of projection systems studied

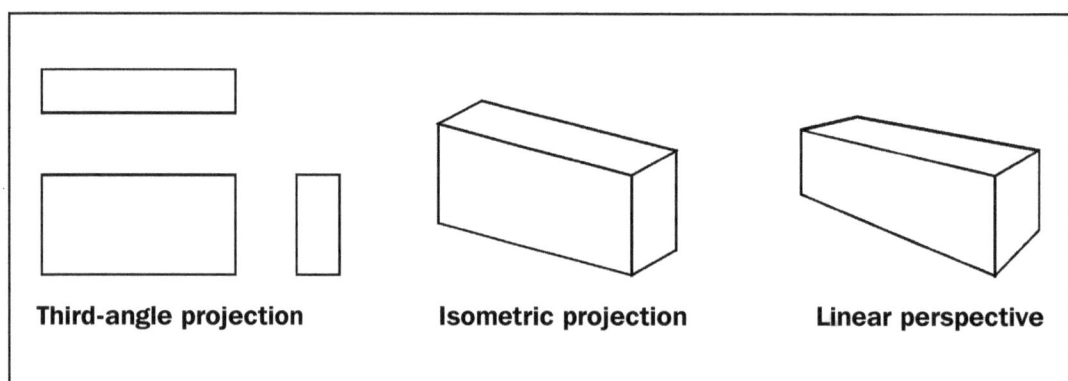

Third-angle projection   Isometric projection   Linear perspective

Chapter 7

Research Methodology

7.1. Introduction

This chapter describes the ways in which the hypotheses presented in Chapter 6 have been tested. Specifically, it presents: the basis of the test design; the principal requirements in experimental technique that were identified and applied to ensure validity of the tests; the pilot test designs and methods, along with a description of the group of subjects who performed the pilot tests; discussions and conclusions relating to each test design; and the revised tests and methods with descriptions of the groups of subjects who performed the revised tests. Figures and photographs for Chapter 7 are presented at the end of the chapter (pp.118-128).

7.2. The basis of the test design

In studying the effect of different methods of pictorial representation on understanding, a definition of what is meant by 'understanding' within the context of the research was considered before the tests were developed. Spencer (1965) notes that here, understanding would best be defined 'in operational terms because the process it denotes involves the extraction of specific items of information from the drawing to achieve a given objective'.

Spencer's definition was adopted on the grounds that performance in extracting specific information from drawings could be measured by asking subjects to undertake a range of tests within a given period of time. Principal requirements in experimental technique were first identified to ensure that the results of the tests would be valid.

7.3. Principal requirements of experimental technique

The following requirements of experimental technique were identified:

- Any task to be set before the subjects should not merely test *recall of knowledge* since this would confuse the information conveyed by a pictorial representation with existing cognitive structures.

- The set tasks must have reasonable face validity, i.e. they must be tolerably similar to actual practical situations in which drawings are used.

- As it is necessary to present drawings composed using different drawing systems to the same subjects, the objects to be represented should be similar so that differences in performance can only be ascribed to the differences between the drawing systems.

- The set tasks should not require special sensory or motor skills. For example, if successful completion of a task were to depend on accurate discrimination of small differences in the drawing, or on manipulative skill, then differences in performance may be due to differences in these abilities and not in pictorial perception.

- Only minimal explanations of the tasks should be necessary. Long explanations could disadvantage subjects whose first language is not that in which the tasks are set.

- The tasks should produce unequivocal and measurable results.

(Adapted from Constable et al., 1988 and Spencer, 1965)

After consideration of the requirements listed above, the following tests were designed and piloted, based on similar tests designed to determine performance in the perception of projection systems, such as those designed by Jude (1983), Owoeye and Smith (1987), and Elsheikh (1995).

A key assumption of this type of test is that the extraction of information from drawings, as described by Spencer (1965), is a critical part of the process of *visualizing* three-dimensional objects. In other words, if the correct visual information is successfully extracted from the drawing (i.e. a *meaning* is attached to the information), a three-dimensional model of the object can be held in the imagination of the viewer. Similarly, if only part of the information is given meaning by the viewer, an incomplete model of the object will be visualized. In extreme circumstances, where no meaning at all is attached to any of the information, the viewer will simply have no idea about the three-dimensional nature of the object represented by the drawing.

7.4. The sample group and pilot tests

The sample group comprised 20 postgraduate students who had recently arrived at WEDC for the start of the 1998-1999 postgraduate programme. Ten subjects were engineers. Ten were non-engineers. Half were of Western origin. They were representative, therefore, of the professional adult learning group described in Chapter 3. A profile of each subject was recorded on the Subject Profile Form (see Appendix 1). Information requested was related to the variables listed in Section 6.4.

All but one of the tests involved the visualization of abstract objects. It was presumed that a task which involved visualizing identifiable objects might influence the results of tests in favour of those subjects familiar with the shape and form of the chosen objects.

None of the objects had been presented to any of the subjects in any form before the tests took place. None of the tasks required special motor skills. Brief explanations of the tasks were provided on the task sheets and were also presented orally.

The pilot tests are described and as follows:

- Pilot Test P1: Third-angle projection – drawing completion task

- Pilot Test P2: Third-angle projection – construction task

- Pilot Test P3: Isometric projection – drawing completion task

- Pilot Test P4: Isometric projection – construction task

- Pilot Test P5: Visualization of plans from isometric projections

- Pilot Test P6: The 'false perspective' task

Tests P1, P3, P5 and P6 were taken during the same session under examination conditions: i.e. none of the subjects was allowed to confer. 16 of the 20 subjects completed the construction tasks (P2 and P4). These were taken individually and under supervision.

7.4.1 Pilot Test P1: Third-angle projection – drawing completion task

7.4.1.1 Purpose

This test was designed to assess the ability of subjects to visualize views of the top and sides of three-dimensional objects.

7.4.1.2 Description

Subjects were referred to Task Sheet P1 (Figure 7.1a: p.118) (Please note that figures for Chapter 7 are presented at the end of the chapter). Contained within each of the boxes (1 to 10) on this sheet is a set of linear projections of three different views of a single solid object. There are views as seen from above (a), from the front (b), and from the right-hand side (c). One or more of the projections from each set is incomplete.

7.4.1.3 Method

The test was conducted under examination conditions, so conferring between subjects was prohibited. Subjects were required to complete the set of projections on the task sheet by adding a full or dashed line (or combination of lines) on the projection or projections they considered to be incomplete. It was noted that a solid line represents the visible meeting of two planes, and that a dashed line represents the hidden meeting of two planes. A time limit of 10 minutes was set. Answers to questions about the task were given on request. Two marks were awarded for each correct answer.

7.4.1.4 Discussion

Observations of this task revealed that some subjects had difficulty in understanding precisely what was required. Most of these difficulties centred around the number of lines necessary to complete the set of projections, and the meaning of the dashed lines. It later transpired that most subjects found this test to be the most difficult. Although this could be attributed, at least in part, to the order in which the tasks were presented (and that this was the first task), it was clear from discussions with those subjects who performed well in all tasks, that P1 was indeed more difficult. Furthermore, the number of lines necessary to complete the set of projections did not equate in all cases to the available marks to be awarded for each set — i.e. two. This led to errors in the scoring system which was based on two marks for a correct answer: one mark for each line completed. Where a set of projections required three lines for completion, subjective judgements had to be made about the relative value of a partial answer. The range of scores for this test was 0-20.

7.4.1.5 Conclusion

It was concluded that revisions should be made so that both the requirements of the task, and the scoring system of subsequent tests, would not be ambiguous. Because most subjects appeared to find this task the most difficult, it was also decided that it should not be the first to be presented in the series.

Despite the reservations and errors described, the range of the results indicated that both the complexity of the task set was appropriate, and that the time allowed was adequate for a revised test, R3 (Figure 7.1b: p.119) to be conducted on a larger scale.

7.4.2 Pilot Test P2: Third-angle projection – construction task

7.4.2.1 Purpose

This test was designed to assess the ability of subjects to visualize the form of abstract objects from third-angle projections.

7.4.2.2 Description

Contained within each of the boxes (1-6) shown on Task Sheet P2 (Figure 7.2a: p.120) is a set of linear projections of three views of a single solid object. With reference to each set of drawings (presented on individual cards one at a time as illustrated in Photograph 7.1: p.126) subjects were invited to construct a model of the object using some or all of the ten wooden components illustrated in Photograph 7.3: p.126.

7.4.2.3 Method

The test was conducted under interview conditions. Subjects performed the task one at a time in an evenly lit room under the supervision of the interviewer. A demonstration was given with an example set of projections, so that subjects clearly understood the requirements of the task. The time taken to construct each model was recorded, with a maximum time limit of 300 seconds (five minutes) allocated for each model.

7.4.2.4 *Discussion*

In the light of the earlier problems experienced with Pilot Test P1, this construction task was performed *after* the isometric version of this task, Pilot Test P4. No help was given in choosing the wooden pieces necessary to complete the task, or by suggesting how the problem of completing the task in the time allocated might be approached.

The range of scores for this test was 0-100. As the maximum number of seconds allocated for completion of each task was 300, marks were awarded according to the scale below. No marks were awarded if the model was incomplete or incorrect after 300 seconds had passed.

No of seconds	% score
300 +	0
286-300	5
271-285	10
256-270	15
241-255	20
226-240	25
211-225	30
196-210	35
181-195	40
176-180	45
151-175	50
136-150	55
121-135	60
106-120	65
91-105	70
76-90	75
61-75	80
46-60	85
31-45	90
16-30	95
0-15	100

The mean average of scores for each of the six models (Photographs 7.4a-7.4f: p.127) was taken and recorded as the percentage score for this task.

7.4.2.5 Conclusion

The tests were carried out on 16 subjects from the group of 20 who completed the drawing completion tasks. There were no apparent problems with understanding what was required. The same instructions were given to each subject. It was concluded that this test had produced valid results.

7.4.3 Pilot Test P3: Isometric projection – drawing completion task

7.4.3.1 Purpose

This test was designed to assess the ability of subjects to visualize isometric projections of three-dimensional objects.

7.4.3.2 Description

Subjects were referred to Task Sheet P3 (Figure 7.3a: p.121). Contained within each of the boxes (1 to 10) on this sheet is an incomplete isometric projection. Without reference to an actual physical object, subjects were asked to complete the projections.

7.4.3.3 Method

As with Pilot Test P1, this test was also conducted under examination conditions. Subjects were required to complete the set of projections on the task sheet by adding a full or dashed line (or combination of lines) on each projection. It was noted that a solid line represents the visible meeting of two planes, and that a dashed line represents the hidden meeting of two planes. A time limit of 10 minutes was set. Answers to questions about the task were given on request. Two marks were awarded for each correct answer.

7.4.3.4 *Discussion*

Observations of this task also revealed that some subjects had difficulty in understanding precisely what was required, and that these difficulties also centred around the number of lines necessary to complete each drawing. Nevertheless, it was generally considered an easier task than the third-angle drawing completion task. There were no errors reported in the construction of the test. Only two straight lines were required to complete each drawing. Although it was noted that the second drawing of this set could be completed in two ways, both were counted as valid answers. The range of scores for this test was 0-20.

7.4.3.5 *Conclusion*

It was concluded that requirements of the task should be made more explicit but that no revisions were required to the design of the task sheet. As subjects appeared to find this test easier than Pilot Test P1 a change in the order of the revised tests seemed appropriate to allow subjects undertaking the revised tests to gain confidence in their performance.

The time allowed for the pilot test was considered adequate for the revised test (R1) to be conducted on a larger scale (Figure 7.3b: p.122).

7.4.4 Pilot Test P4: Isometric projection – construction task

7.4.4.1 *Purpose*

This test was designed to assess the ability of subjects to visualize the physical shape of abstract objects from isometric projections.

7.4.4.2 *Description*

The description of this task is similar to the description of Pilot Test P2. Contained within each of the boxes (1-6) shown on Task Sheet P4 (Figure 7.4: p.123) is an isometric projection of a single solid object.

With reference to each drawing (presented on individual cards one at a time illustrated in Photograph 7.2: p.126) subjects were invited to construct a model of the object using some or all of the same ten wooden components used for Task P2 illustrated in Photograph 7.3: p.126.

7.4.4.3 Method

The test was conducted under interview conditions. In the light of the experience gained by conducting Pilot Tests P1 and P3 (the drawing completion tasks) this construction task (P4) was presented to subjects *before* Pilot Test P2.

Subjects performed this task during the same session as Task P2. A demonstration of this task was also given with an example set of projections, so that subjects clearly understood the requirements of the task. The time taken to construct each model was recorded, with the same maximum time limit of 300 seconds (five minutes) as Task P2 allocated for each model.

7.4.4.4 Discussion

As with Pilot Test P2, no help was given in choosing the wooden pieces necessary to complete the task, or by suggesting how the problem of completing the task in time allocated might be approached.

The same scoring system described in Section 7.4.2.4 was used. The mean average of the scores for each of the six models was taken and recorded as the percentage score for this task (Photographs 7.5a-7.5f: p.128).

7.4.4.5 Conclusion

As in the case of Pilot Test P2, Pilot Test P4 was performed by the same 16 subjects from the group of 20 who completed the drawing completion tasks. There were no apparent problems in understanding the requirements of the test. The same instructions were given to each subject. It was concluded that this test had also produced valid results.

7.4.5 Pilot Test P5: Visualization of plans from isometric projections

7.4.5.1 Purpose
This test was designed to assess the ability of a subject to visualize the plan of an abstract object from an isometric projection of the object.

7.4.5.2 Description
Contained within each of the boxes (1-10) on Task Sheet P5 (Figure 7.5: p.124) is an isometric drawing of a single solid object.

For this test, subjects were invited to refer to each set of drawings one at a time and to sketch (on the paper provided) a linear representation of each object as though seen directly from above.

7.4.5.3 Method
As with Pilot Tests P1 and P3, this test was conducted under examination conditions. A time limit of 10 minutes was set and answers to questions about the task were given on request. Two marks were awarded for each correct answer. A single discretionary mark was awarded when it was clear that some, but not all aspects of the plan view had been visualized. Only a schematic representation of the plan was required. Full marks were awarded, therefore, even though the dimensions of the sketch may have appeared disproportionate to the isometric projection. It was presumed that discounting marks on these grounds would have penalised subjects who possessed poorer drawing skills, but who had nevertheless visualized the plan correctly.

7.4.5.4 Discussion
Whereas Pilot Tests P1 and P3 focussed on particular types of projection (i.e. either third-angle or isometric), this task demanded an understanding of both: isometric projection for interpreting the physical nature of the object represented, and third-angle projection for visualizing a schematic mental image of the plan.

7.4.5.5 Conclusion

No problems were reported with either the design of the test, nor with understanding the requirements of the test. Although an element of discretion described above was involved during marking, it was not considered to be significant to invalidate the results.

7.4.6 Pilot Test P6: Perspective – the 'false perspective' task

7.4.6.1 Purpose

This test was designed to assess whether subjects recognised the laws of linear perspective as a primary means of defining pictorial space.

7.4.6.2 Description

Pictured on Task Sheet P6 (Figure 7.6: p.125) is a copy of an engraving by William Hogarth, an eighteenth century English artist. Hogarth constructed this picture and called it 'False perspective' to illustrate ambiguities in the representation of pictorial space when the laws for defining space in illustrations are deliberately broken. The result is an image which contains illogical situations that could not exist or happen in reality.

7.4.6.3 Method

Subjects were each provided with a photocopy of Hogarth's etching. By circling areas of the photocopy with a pen and adding annotations, subjects were invited to locate and describe situations in the picture which they believed could not take place in the real world. This was demonstrated with an example. The horizon line as described by water, and usually represented at a 90 degree angle to the vertical edge of the image area, appears to slope steeply.

The principal features of Hogarth's picture which appeared to break the laws of pictorial space were identified and grouped as follows:

112

Group A: Perspective as defined by the rules of linear perspective

Examples:

- Both ends of the church can be seen. According to the rules of linear perspective, only one should be visible.

- The vanishing point for the windows of the building in the foreground recede to a point somewhere in the sky, and not to the horizon line.

- The vanishing point of the tiles of the floor on which the nearest angler is standing appears to recede to a point below the area of the picture, and not to the horizon line.

- The horizon line is not horizontal.

- The vanishing point of the panels of the nearest elevation of the building in the foreground do not recede to a consistent vanishing point.

Group B: Perspective as defined by the size/position relationship of picture elements

Examples:

- The man on the distant hill looks as large as the woman leaning out of the window of the inn.

- The trees on the hill appear to become larger the farther their distance from the viewer.

- The bridge does not appear to span the river.

- The bird in the distance appears too large for the tree on which it is perched.

- The swan appears bigger than the cattle shown in a nearer plane.

Group C: Perspective as defined by spatial planes

Examples:

- The man on the distant hill appears to be lighting his pipe from the candle of the woman leaning out of the window of the inn which is situated in the foreground.

- Two of the trees on the hill in the distance overlap the inn sign which is situated on a plane nearer to the viewer.

- The anglers' lines interfere with each other, even though the anglers are separated by distance.

- The man in the boat on the river beyond the bridge appears to be shooting into the distance, whilst smoke from the gun floats in front of the bridge.

- The struts of the inn sign are located on buildings situated in different planes.

Subjects were awarded a score of A, B, or C or a combination of these letters according to whether or not they identified illogical elements of the drawing as categorized above. For example, if a subject identified elements from all groups, a score of ABC would be recorded. If only features from two groups were identified then either a score of AB, BC or AC would be recorded. If features from only one group were identified, a result of A, B, or C would be recorded. Only one feature for each group was required to be identified for a score to be awarded.

7.4.6.4 Discussion

It was not intended that this test should generate empirical data in the same way as the other pilot tests. As an experimental test, it was performed to see whether trends in the perception of the basic spatial cues in pictures could be identified. Subjects scoring A, B and C, for example, might be said to perceive pictorial space in a number of different ways. Subjects scoring only a C, however, might be said to depend more for their perception of pictorial space on the depiction of spatial planes than on the size/position relationship of drawing elements, or on linear perspective.

The context of Hogarth's picture also has an important bearing on the validity of this test. The scene is set in eighteenth century England. Subjects unfamiliar with the cultural background of eighteenth century England were faced with additional problems of interpretation and were therefore disadvantaged. For some subjects, for example, the dress code of the angler in the foreground was as much of an issue of misrepresentation as the other features described and grouped above.

7.4.6.5 Conclusion

With the reservations outlined here in mind, it was nevertheless concluded that the results of this test might present an additional insight into the ways in which space is perceived by the different subject groups, and so was carried forward to comprise one of the revised tests.

7.5. The revised tests

The revised tests are listed below. Each has a reference to the pilot test from which it was adapted.

- Revised Test R1 (P3): Isometric projection – drawing completion task

- Revised Test R2 (P5): Visualization of plans from isometric projections

- Revised Test R3 (P1): Third-angle projection – drawing completion task

- Revised Test R4 (P6): Perspective – the 'false perspective' task

- Revised Test R5 (P2): Isometric projection – construction task

- Revised Test R6 (P4): Third-angle projection – construction task

The revised tests were performed by a range of adult learning groups. Although they were completed at different times and locations, it was possible to apply the same conditions for each of the groups. In two instances (noted in Table 7.1 below) the tests were successfully introduced and co-ordinated by other people, demonstrating that the tests are replicable. The Subject Profile Form (see Appendix 1) had been adapted to include details of both handedness and dyslexia as potentially additional influential variables on the results. Other significant variables related to the profiles of subjects as listed below in Section 6.4 had been previously agreed with the research supervisors. Categories for each variable are given in Table 7.2.

Table 7.1. Description of subject groups and locations of the tests

Subject group	Description	No of subjects	Location
a	WEDC postgraduate students	33	Loughborough, UK
b	Civil Engineering postgraduate students	20	Loughborough, UK
c*	Civil Engineering undergraduate students	27	Loughborough, UK
d	LUSAD pre-degree students	20	Loughborough, UK
e*	NUST Civil Engineering undergraduate students	20	Bulawayo, Zimbabwe

c*   Test led by Dr David Twigg, Joint Research Supervisor, Department of Civil and Building Engineering, Loughborough University, UK.

e*   Test led by the Dean of Engineering, National University for Science and Technology, (NUST) Bulawayo, Zimbabwe.

116

Table 7.2. Variables and categories

Variable	Categories
Subject group	As listed in Table 7.1
Age	Under 20 21-30 31-40 41-50 51-60 61 or over
Artistic background	Yes No
Country of birth	Not limited
Country of childhood	Not limited
Country of education	Not limited
Country of permanent residence	Not limited
Dyslexia	Yes No
Educational level	Pre-degree Undergraduate Postgraduate
English is first language	Yes No
Ethnic origin	Not limited
Formal training in engineering drawing or technical illustration	None 1-3 4-6 7-9 Over 10
Gender	Male Female
Handedness	Left Right Ambidextrous
Nationality	Not limited
Professional status	1 of 4 options
Quality of sight	Adequate/good Poor
Region	Low-income country High-income country
Religious background	Not limited
Work experience	Under 5 5-10 11-15 21-25 26-30 31 or over

The following chapter presents the results of the tests.

Figure 7.1a Task Sheet P1

Task Sheet P1

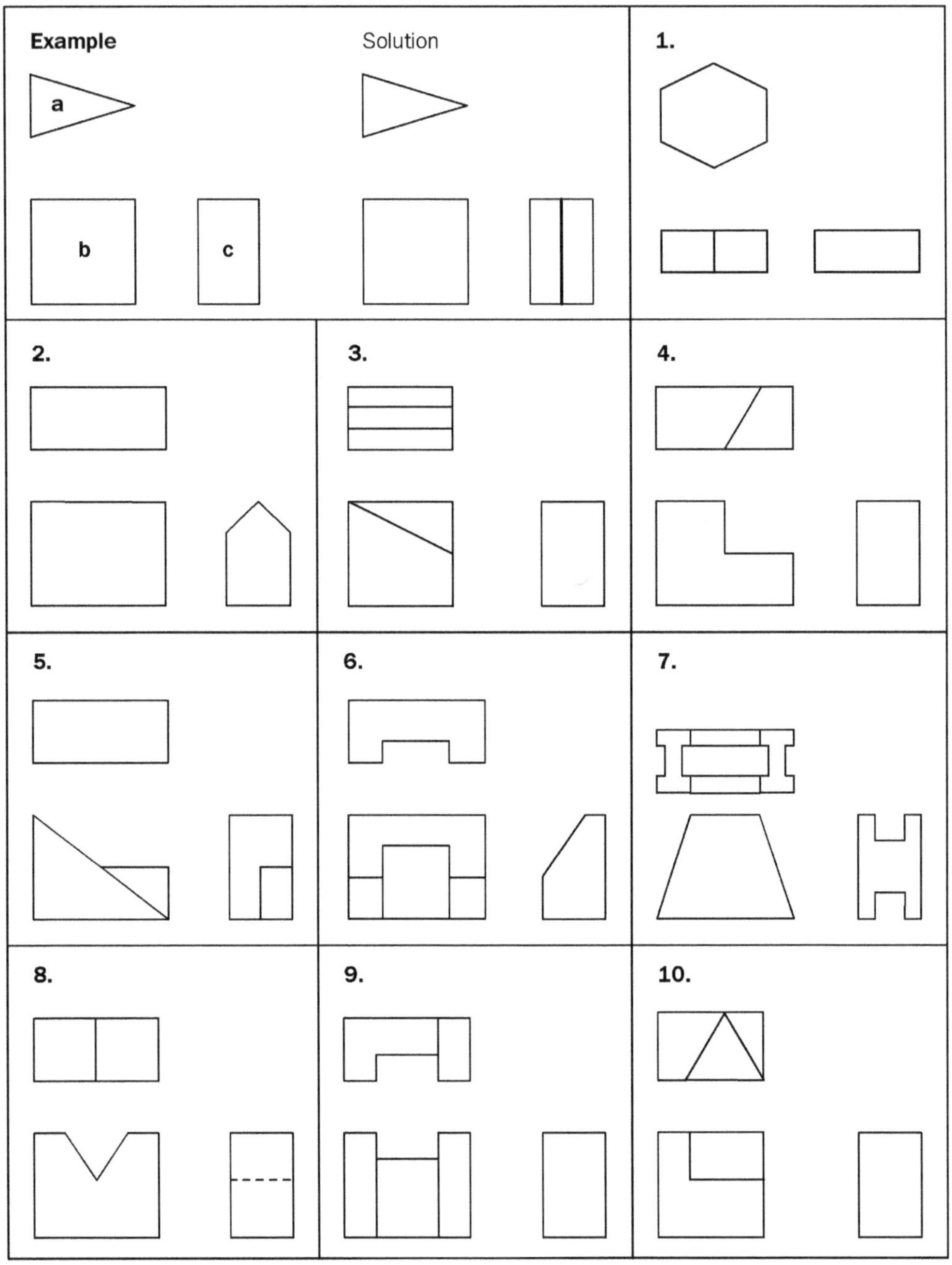

Figure 7.1b   Task Sheet R3

Task Sheet R3

Name: _____ Date: _____ Ref. No. _____

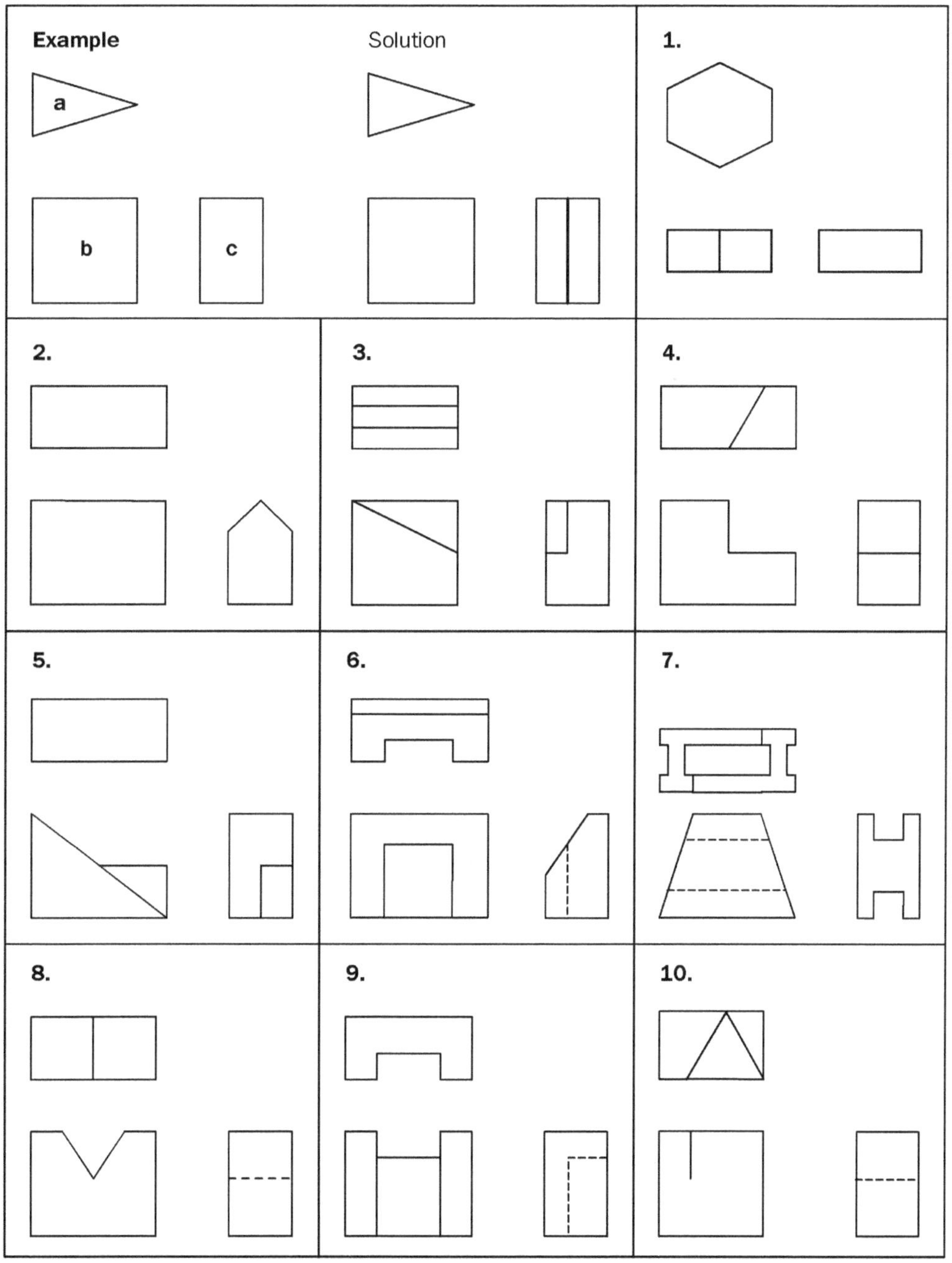

Figure 7.2. Task Sheet P2 (later Task Sheet R6)

120

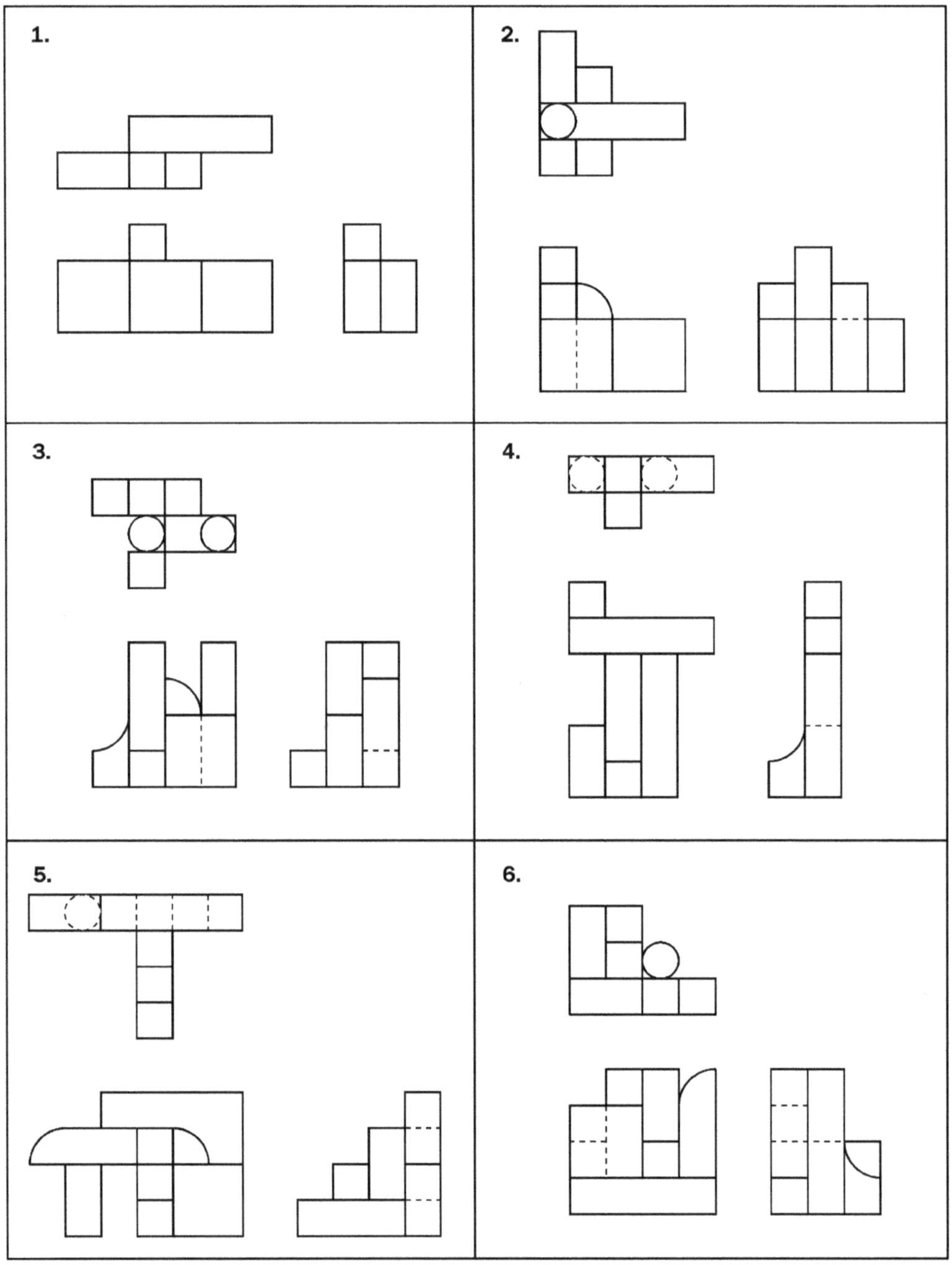

Figure 7.3a   Task Sheet P3

Task Sheet P3

Name: _____ Date: _____ Ref. No. _____

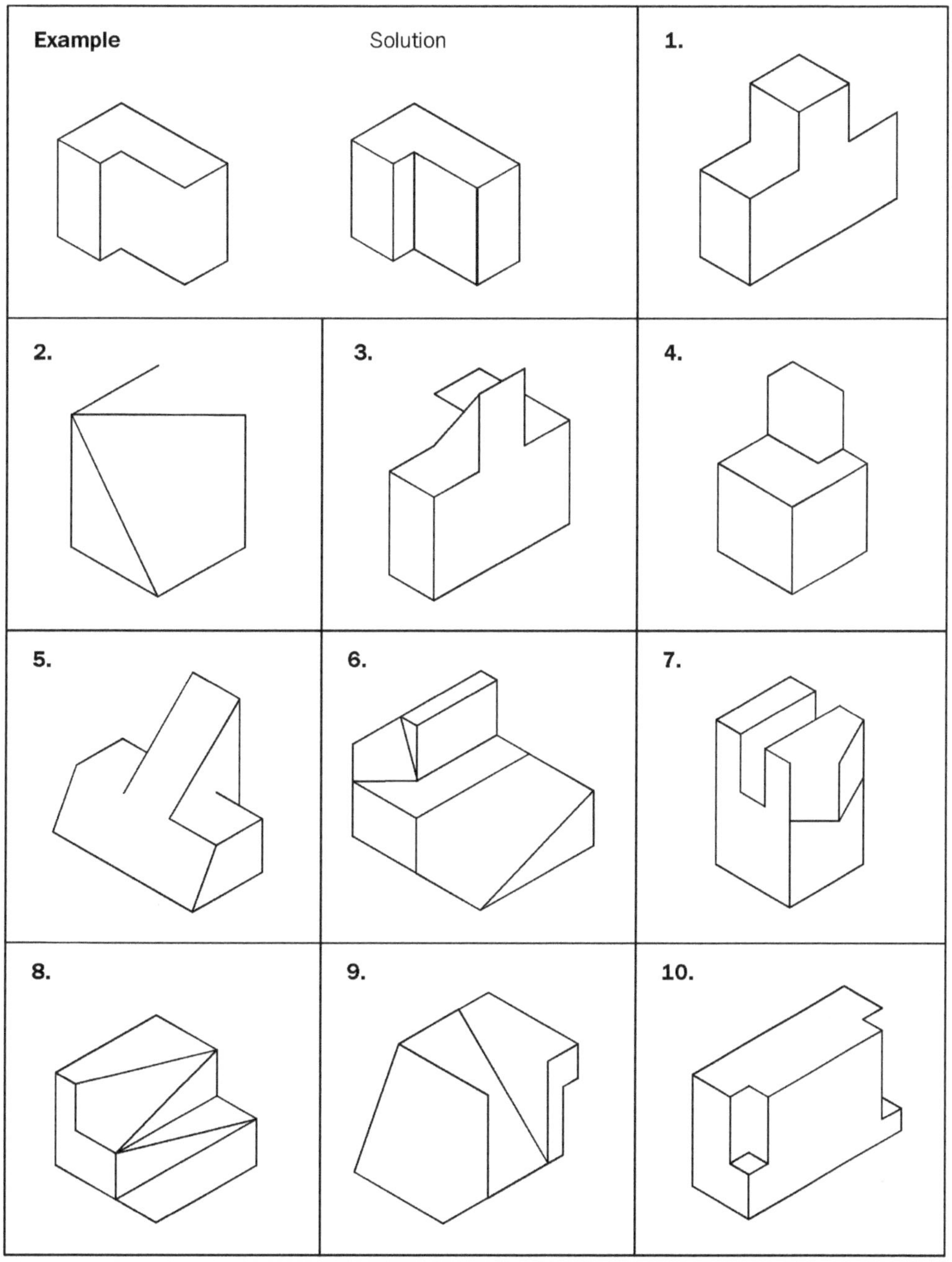

Example / Solution		1.
2.	3.	4.
5.	6.	7.
8.	9.	10.

121

Figure 7.3b Task Sheet R1

Task Sheet R1

Name: _____ Date: _____ Ref. No. _____

Example	Solution	1.
2.	3.	4.
5.	6.	7.
8.	9.	10.

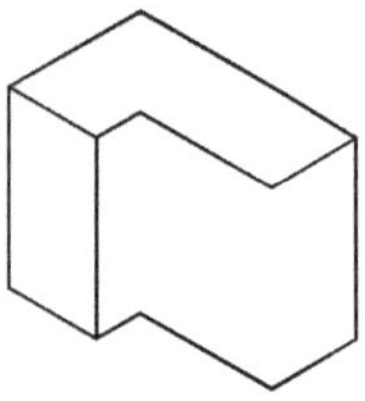

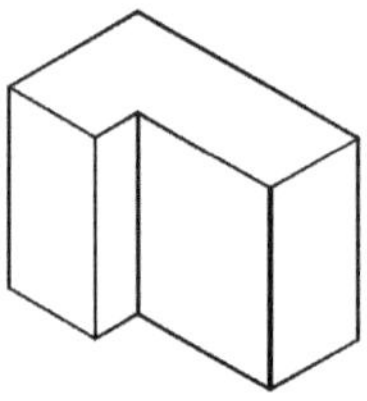

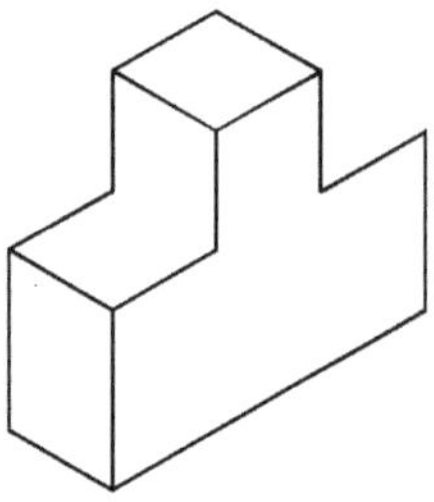

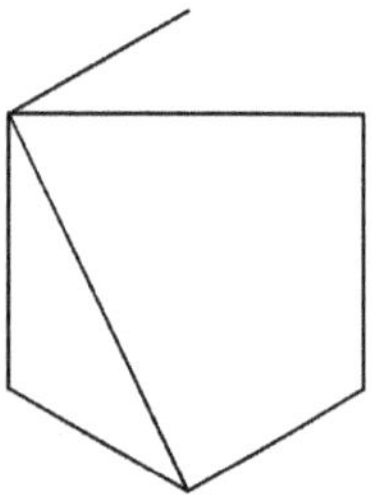

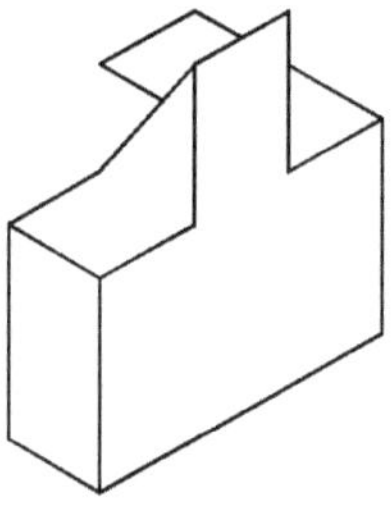

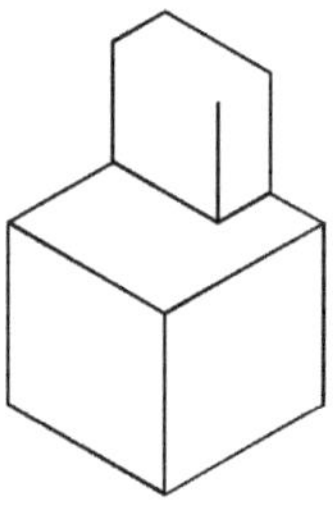

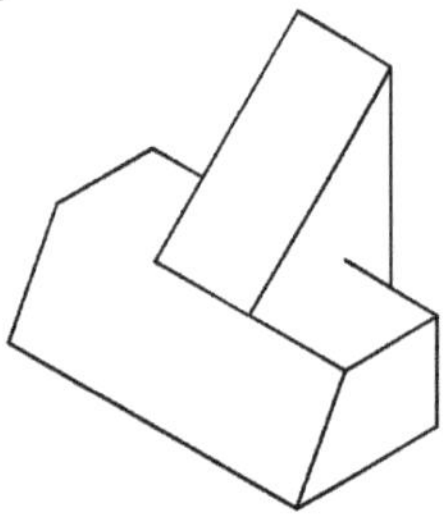

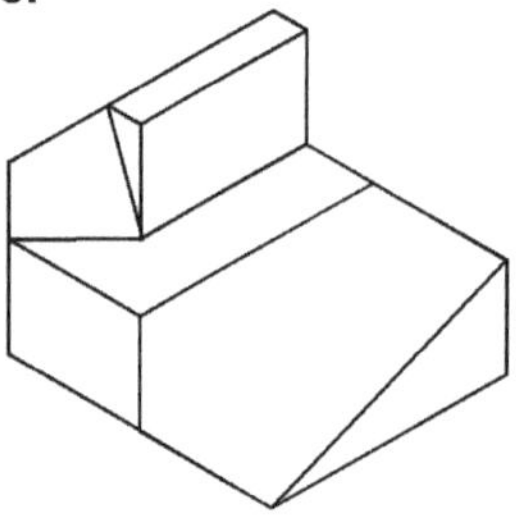

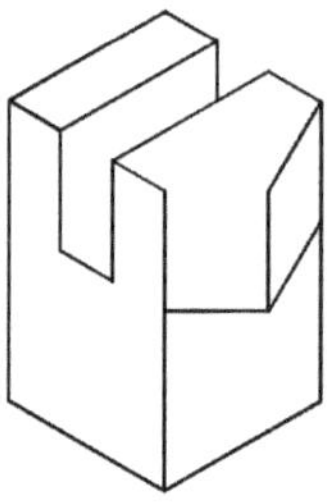

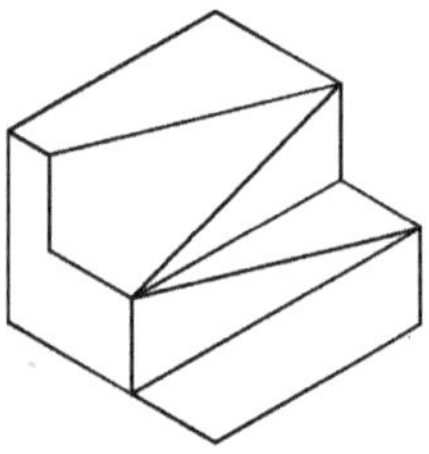

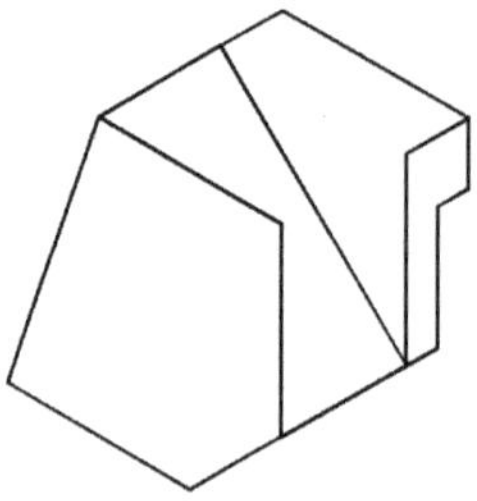

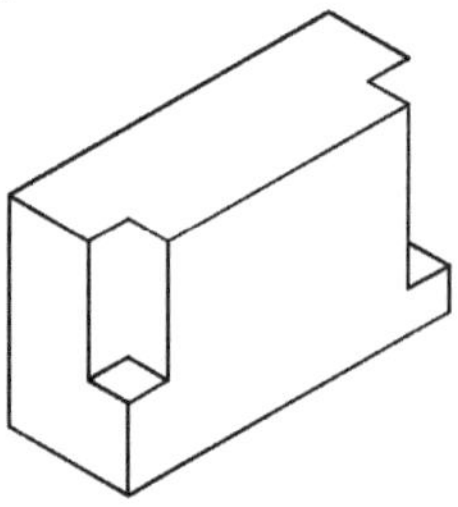

Figure 7.4. Task Sheet P4 (later Task Sheet R5)

Task Sheet P4

Name: _____ Date: _____ Ref. No. _____

1.

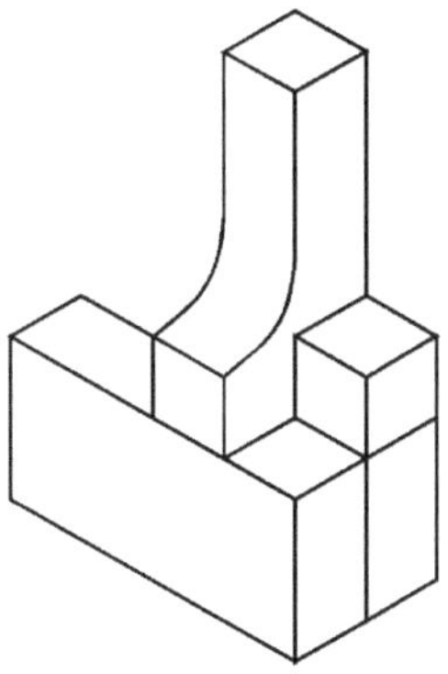

2.

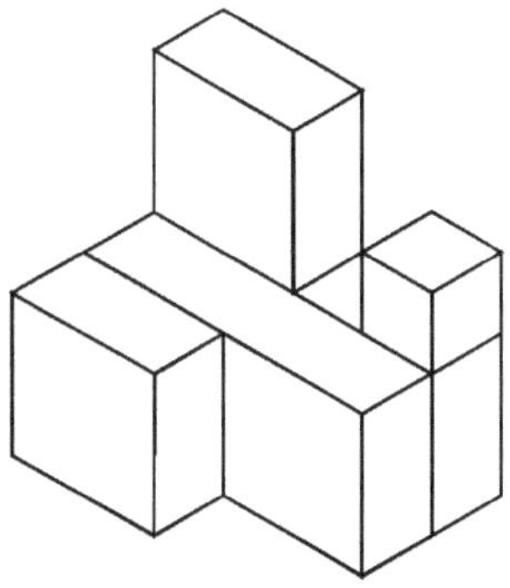

3.

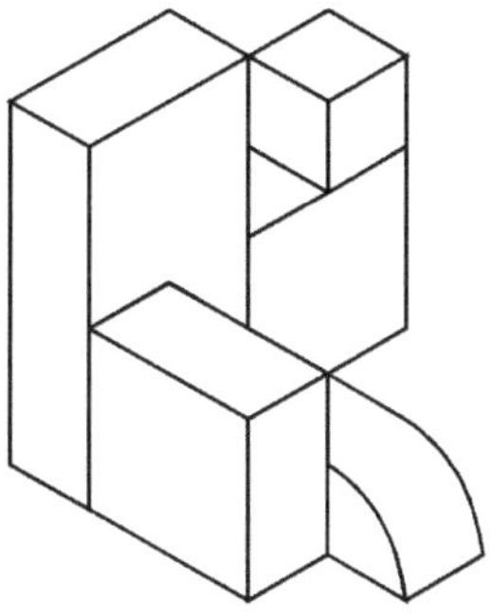

4.

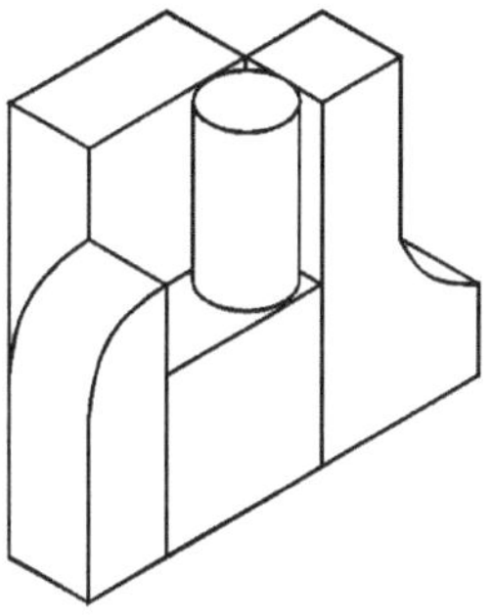

5.

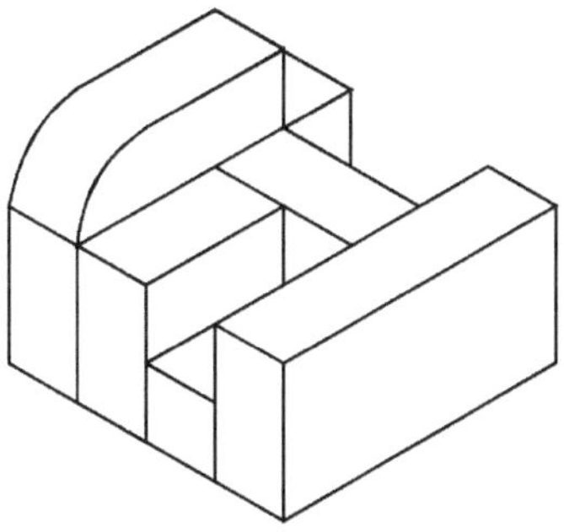

6.

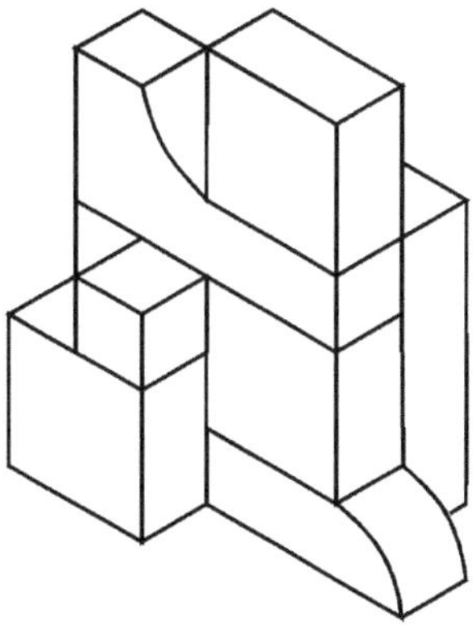

123

Figure 7.5. Task Sheet P5 (later Task Sheet R2)

Task Sheet P5

Name: _____ Date: _____ Ref. No. _____

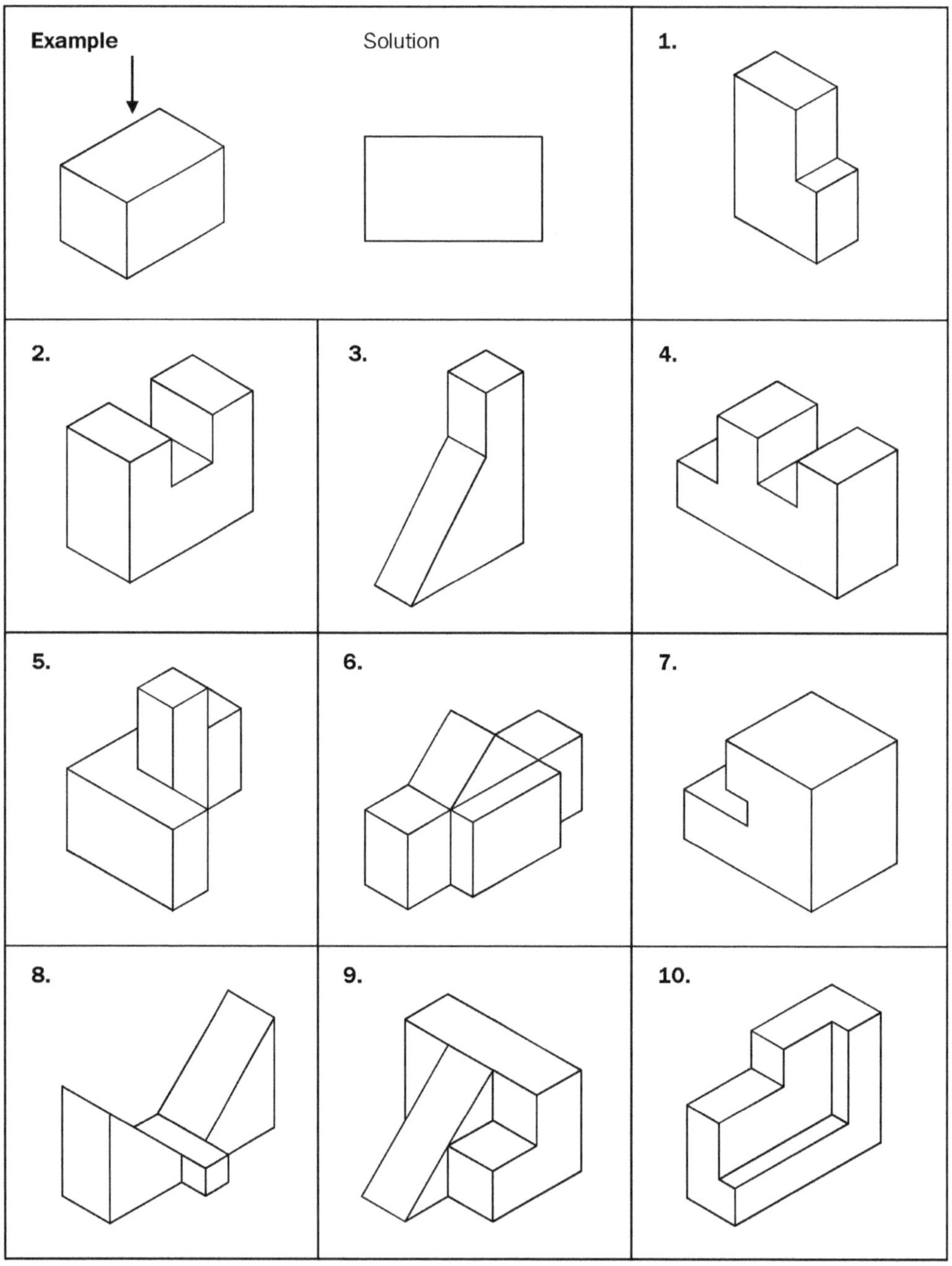

Figure 7.6. Task Sheet P6 (later Task Sheet R4)

Task Sheet P6

Name: _____ Date: _____ Ref. No. _____

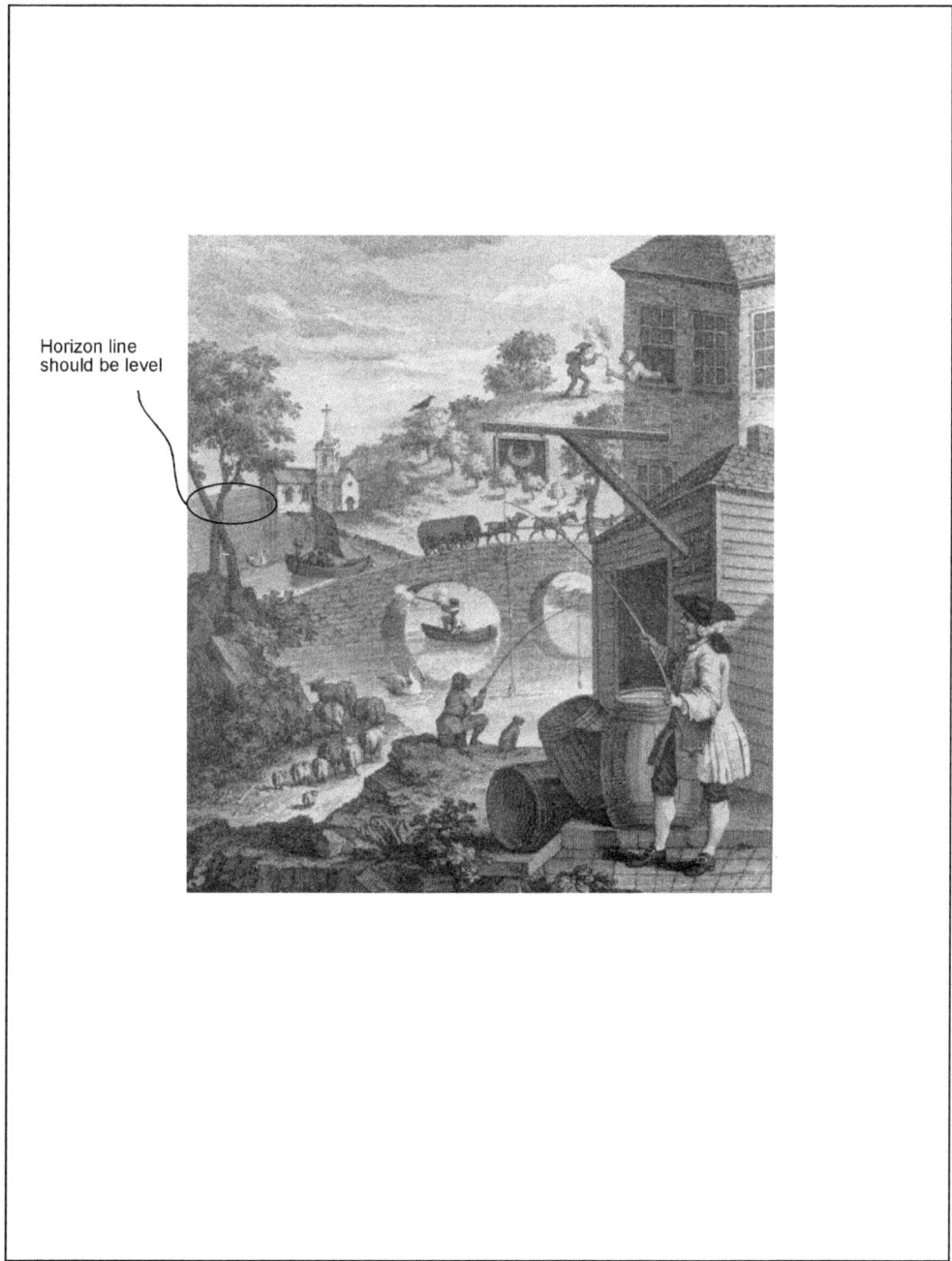

Horizon line
should be level

Photograph 7.1. **Task card for the third-angle projection construction task P2**

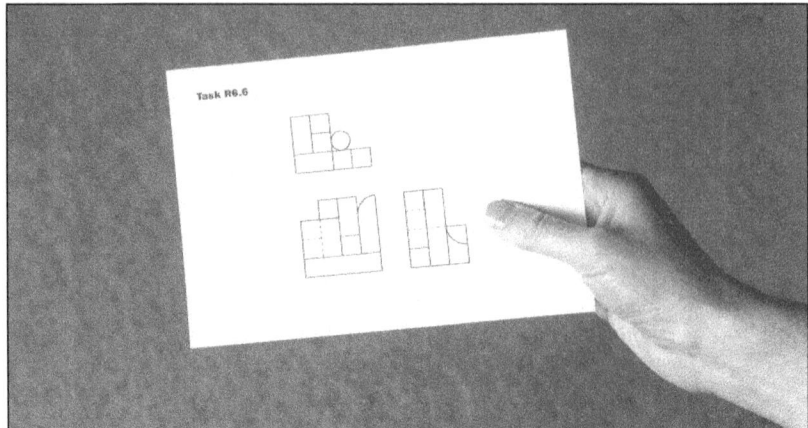

Photograph 7.2. **Task card for the isometric projection construction task P4**

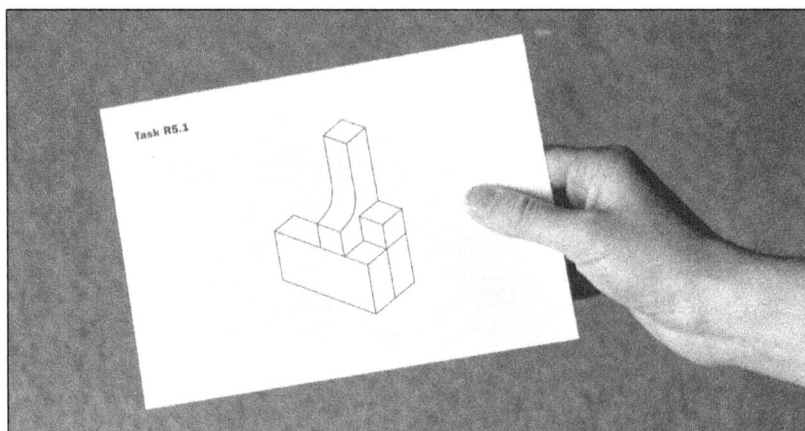

Photograph 7.3. **Wooden components for constructing models for Tasks P2 and Tasks P4**

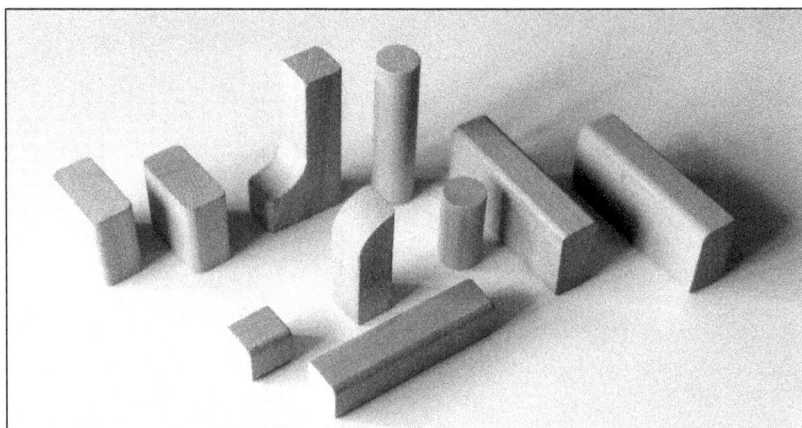

Photographs 7.4. Correct solutions for the third-angle projection construction tasks (P2) (R6)

a

b

c

d

e

f

Photographs 7.5. Correct solutions for the isometric projection
construction tasks (P4) (R5)

a

b

c

d

e

f

Chapter 8

Results

8.1. Introduction

Data compiled from the Subject Profile Forms (Appendix 1) were entered into the statistical analysis and data management system SPSS, along with the scores for the pilot tests (where these were considered valid) and the revised tests. This chapter presents a summary of the results of the revised tests in tabular and chart form. Figures for Chapter 8 are presented at the end of the chapter.

Analysis and discussion of the data is presented in Chapter 9.

8.2. Frequency tables

This section lists frequencies by variables beginning with *Subject group*, then alphabetically by variable name.

Table 8.1. Subject group frequency table

Subject group		Frequency	Per cent
WEDC postgraduate students	(Group a)	33	27.5
Civil Engineering postgraduate students	(Group b)	20	16.7
Civil Engineering undergraduate students	(Group c)	27	22.5
LUSAD pre-degree students	(Group d)	20	16.7
NUST undergraduate students	(Group e)	20	16.7
Total		**120**	**100.0**

Table 8.2. Age frequency table

Age	Frequency	Per cent
15-20	43	35.8
21-30	51	42.5
31-40	20	16.7
41-50	5	4.2
Missing	1	0.8
Total	**120**	**100.0**

Table 8.3. Artistic background frequency table

Artistic background	Frequency	Per cent
No	92	76.7
Yes	28	23.3
Total	**120**	**100.0**

Table 8.4. Country of birth frequency table

Country of birth	Frequency	Per cent
Australia	1	0.8
Brunei	1	0.8
France	2	1.7
Germany	1	0.8
Ghana	1	0.8
Greece	1	0.8
Hong Kong	1	0.8
Indonesia	1	0.8
Ireland	2	1.7
Jamaica	1	0.8
Japan	3	2.5
Kenya	3	2.5
Liberia	1	0.8
Libya	1	0.8
Malawi	1	0.8
Namibia	1	0.8
Nigeria	3	2.5
Oman	1	0.8

Pakistan	2	1.7
Papua New Guinea	1	0.8
Philippines	1	0.8
Portugal	1	0.8
Singapore	1	0.8
St Vincent	1	0.8
The Netherlands	3	2.5
Uganda	3	2.5
UK	57	47.5
Uzbekistan	1	0.8
Vietnam	1	0.8
Zambia	1	0.8
Zimbabwe	21	17.5
Total	**120**	**100.0**

Table 8.5. Dyslexia frequency table

Dyslexia	Frequency	Per cent
No	105	87.5
Yes	10	8.3
Missing	5	4.2
Total	**120**	**100.0**

Table 8.6. Educational level frequency table

Educational level	Frequency	Per cent
Pre-degree	20	16.7
Undergraduate	47	39.2
Postgraduate	53	44.2
Total	**120**	**100.0**

Table 8.7. English as first language frequency table

English as first language	Frequency	Per cent
No	57	47.5
Yes	63	52.5
Total	**120**	**100.0**

Table 8.8. Ethnic origin frequency table

Ethnic origin	Frequency	Per cent
African	36	30.0
Asian	11	9.2
Australasian	1	0.8
Central American	2	1.7
Chinese	3	2.5
European	64	53.3
Japanese	2	1.7
Middle Eastern	1	0.8
Total	**120**	**100.0**

Table 8.9. Formal training in engineering drawing / technical illustration

No. years training	Frequency	Per cent
0	47	39.2
1-3	52	43.3
4-6	12	10.0
7-9	2	1.7
10+	7	5.8
Total	**120**	**100.0**

Table 8.10. Gender frequency table

Gender	Frequency	Per cent
Female	27	22.5
Male	93	77.5
Total	**120**	**100.0**

Table 8.11. Handedness frequency table

Handedness	Frequency	Per cent
Ambidextrous	1	0.8
Left-handed	15	12.5
Right-handed	101	84.2
Missing	3	2.5
Total	**120**	**100.0**

Table 8.12. Professional status frequency table

Professional status	Frequency	Per cent
Architect/Planner/Surveyor	3	2.5
Engineer	85	70.8
Non-technologist	28	23.3
Scientist	4	3.3
Total	**120**	**100.0**

Table 8.13. Region (economic) frequency table

Economic region	Frequency	Per cent
High-income country	73	60.8
Low-income country	47	39.2
Total	**120**	**100.0**

Table 8.14. Religious background frequency table

Religious background	Frequency	Per cent
Buddhist	3	2.5
Bahai	1	0.8
Christian	101	84.2
Hindu	3	2.5
Moslem	9	7.5
Missing	3	2.5
Total	**120**	**100.0**

Table 8.15. Work experience frequency table

No. of years work experience	Frequency	Per cent
0-5	90	75.0
5-10	16	13.3
11-15	8	6.7
16-20	1	0.8
21-25	2	1.7
26-30	1	0.8
31+	1	0.8
Missing	1	0.8
Total	**120**	**100.0**

8.3. Selected variables and clustered categories

A number of variables are not listed in Section 8.2 above. The variable *Quality of sight* is not listed as only one subject noted that his eyesight was poor rather than adequate or good. Other subjects noted that they required spectacles to see properly. In such cases, eyesight was regarded as adequate or good for the purpose of completing the tests.

Similarly, the frequency tables for *Nationality*, *Country of childhood*, *Country of education*, and *Country of permanent residence* are not presented here (or considered in the data analysis and discussion which follows) as only three subjects reported differences between these variables and their country of birth. This should not be taken to mean that such variables would not significantly affect the results of tests conducted on a larger scale, but rather that it is not possible to take account of them in analysing the results of these tests, conducted on a small scale, where the data recorded for these variables are minimal.

It is also evident from the frequency tables that study of *Religious background* (Table 8.14) will not yield reliable results. Approximately 84 per cent of subjects declared their religious background to be Christian. Other religious backgrounds included Bahai, Buddhist, Hindu and Moslem which collectively comprised only 14.3 per cent. Larger tests where samples are drawn equally from populations of different religious backgrounds would reveal the level of significance of this variable.

It can be seen from the frequency tables that each variable is comprised of a different number of categories, according to the nature of the variable. Whilst *Gender*, for example, is comprised of only two categories, *Country of birth* is comprised of many. In the latter case, the problem of the scale of the samples described above in relation to the number of categories is also apparent.

For these reasons, variables for analysis and discussion in Chapter 9 have been selected from the initial list, and categories within some of the variables have been grouped together.

Table 9.3 lists the variables and categories which have been selected for analysis and discussion.

8.4. Test scores

The scores are presented here according to the nature of the data for each test. Tests R1, R2, R3, R5 and R6 produced percentage marks, scored on an interval scale. Test R4 produced nominal data.

8.4.1 Interval results for R1, R2 R3, R5, and R6

Table 8.16. Case processing summary for R1, R2, R3, R5, and R6

	Cases					
	Included		Excluded		Total	
	N	Per cent	N	Per cent	N	Per cent
R1	100	83.3%	20	16.7%	120	100.0%
R2	99	82.5%	21	17.5%	120	100.0%
R3	97	80.8%	23	19.2%	120	100.0%
R5	16	13.3%	104	86.7%	120	100.0%
R6	16	13.3%	104	86.7%	120	100.0%

Table 8.17. Case summaries for R1, R2, R3, R5, and R6

	R1	R2	R3	R5	R6
N	100	99	97	16	16
Mean	87.35	89.34	59.95	85.31	38.44
Std. error of mean	1.62	2.03	3.05	4.82	7.51
Minimum	25	0	0	20	0
Maximum	100	100	100	95	80
Range	75	100	100	75	80
Std. deviation	16.21	20.16	30.01	19.28	30.04

135

Figures 8.1 (R1), 8.2 (R2), 8.3 (R3), 8.4 (R5) and 8.5 (R6) for graphical representations of these results.

8.4.2 Nominal results for R4

Table 8.18. Frequencies of scores A, B and C for Test R4

Valid	Frequency	Per cent	Valid Per cent
AB	2	1.7	1.7
ABC	70	58.3	58.8
AC	4	3.3	3.4
B	3	2.5	2.5
BC	33	27.5	27.7
C	7	5.8	5.9
Total	**119**	**99.2**	**100.0**
Missing	1	0.8	
Total	120	100.0	

Table 8.19. Frequencies with and without score A for Test R4

Valid	Frequency	Percent	Valid Percent
Contains A	76	63.3	63.9
Does not contain A	43	35.8	36.1
Total	**119**	**99.2**	**100.0**
Missing	1	0.8	
Total	120	100.0	

See Figures 8.6a and 8.6b (R4) for graphical representations of these results.

Figure 8.1   Test results for Task R1

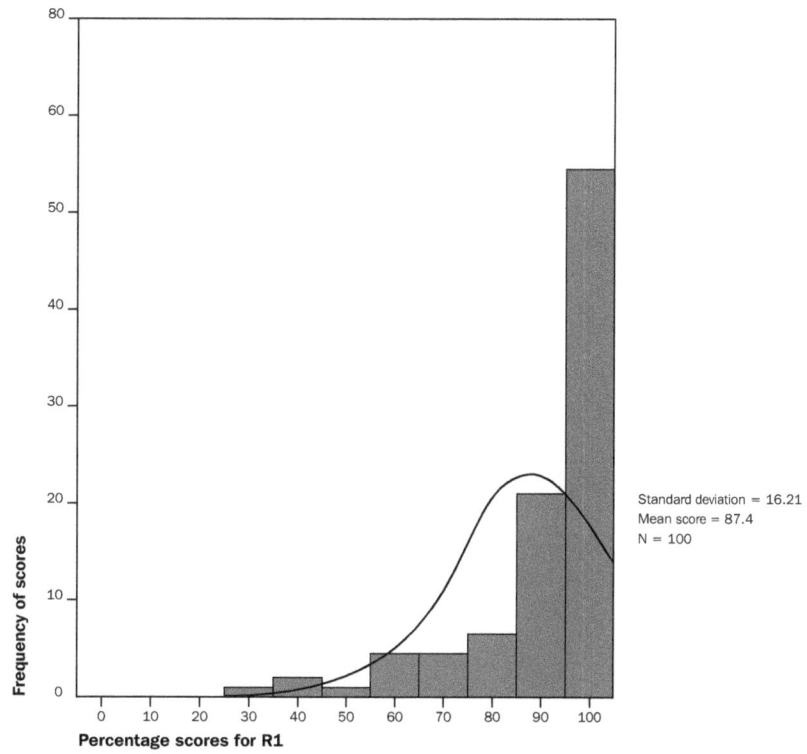

Standard deviation = 16.21
Mean score = 87.4
N = 100

Frequency of scores

Percentage scores for R1

Figure 8.2   Test results for Task R2

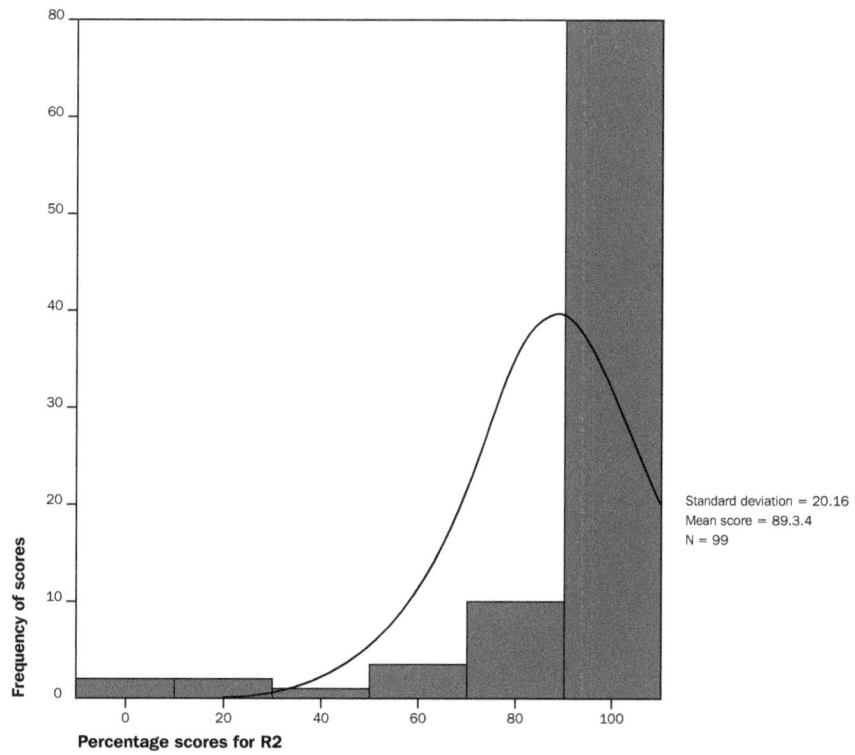

Standard deviation = 20.16
Mean score = 89.3.4
N = 99

Frequency of scores

Percentage scores for R2

Figure 8.3   Test results for Task R3

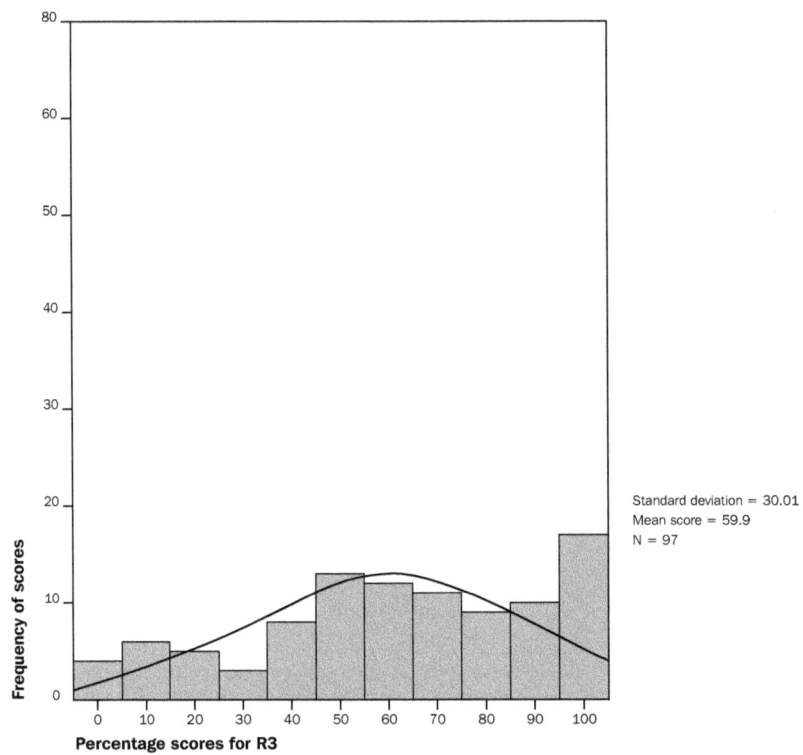

Standard deviation = 30.01
Mean score = 59.9
N = 97

Figure 8.4   Test results for Task R5

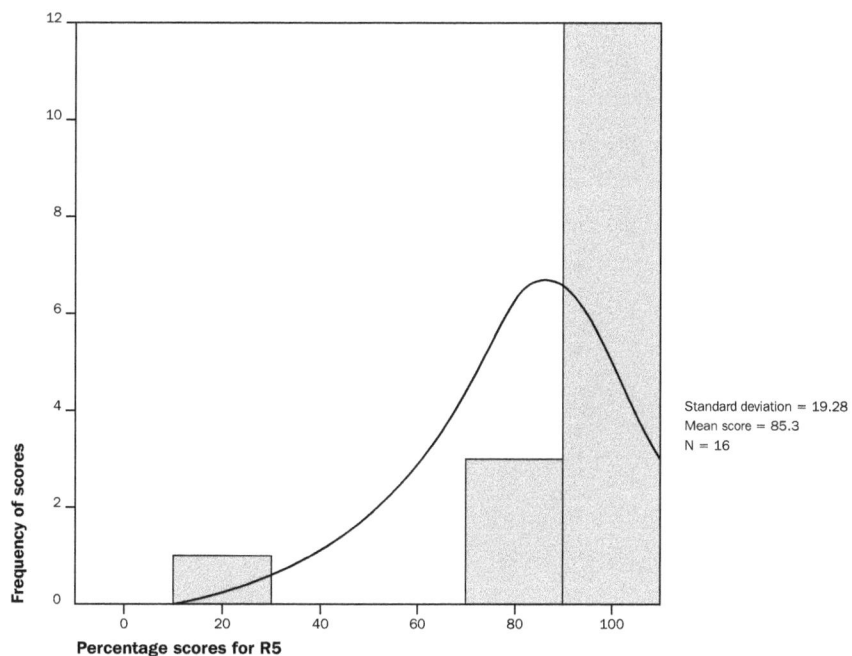

Standard deviation = 19.28
Mean score = 85.3
N = 16

Frequency of scores

Percentage scores for R5

Figure 8.5   Test results for Task R6

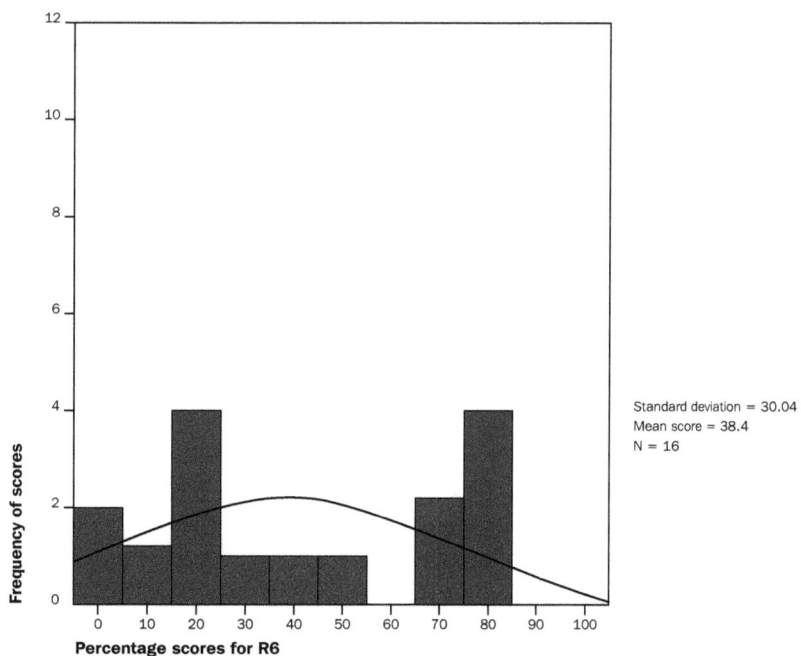

Standard deviation = 30.04
Mean score = 38.4
N = 16

Frequency of scores

Percentage scores for R6

Figure 8.6a   Test results for Task R4 (all groups)

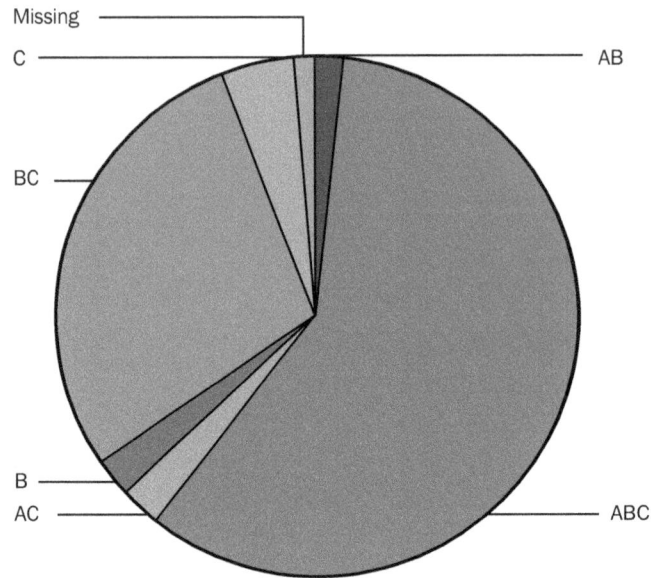

Figure 8.6b   Test results for Task R4 (containing or not containing A)

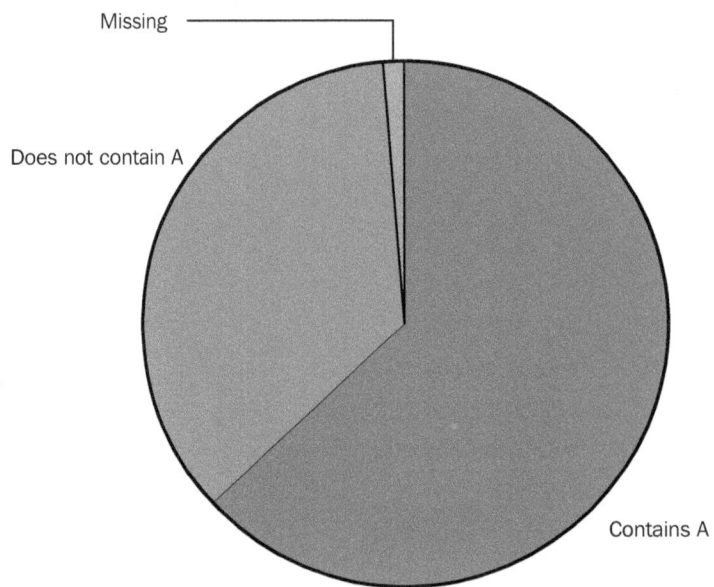

Chapter 9

Data Analysis and Discussion

9.1. Introduction

Chapter 8 presented data from the results of the revised tests. This chapter presents a comparative analysis of the tests themselves, followed by analyses of the results for selected variables and categories. The results are analysed in this way as a means of either supporting or rejecting the hypotheses presented in Chapter 6. Sections in this chapter relating to the each hypothesis are marked in parentheses: i.e. (H1), (H2), and (H3). The extent to which analysis of the data can support or reject the hypotheses is discussed within each section.

Where computation of the levels of statistical difference is thought to be appropriate, non-parametric techniques of hypothesis testing have been used as these methods do not assume that the scores under analysis are drawn from a population distributed in a certain way — such as from a normally distributed population. They are also useful with small samples (Siegel, 1966; Cohen and Holliday, 1984).

Please note that figures for Chapter 9 are presented at the end of this chapter. Inferences and conclusions drawn from these analyses are presented in Chapter 10.

9.2. Comparative analysis of the tests (H1)

Tests R1 and R3 were designed to assess ability in understanding isometric projections and third-angle projections respectively. Tests R5 and R6 were designed to corroborate the results of R1 and R3.

A comparison of the test results R1 and R3 (as presented in Figures 8.1: p.137 and 8.3: p.138) and R5 and R6 (as presented in Figures 8.4 and 8.5: p.139) would reflect similarities and differences in the levels of understanding of the two types of projection if the tests themselves are comparable. It is assumed here that this is true, given that the requirements for completing the tests are the same: i.e. the addition of two lines to each drawing within the same specified period of time. Chapter 7 has discussed the development of the tests in greater detail.

Figures 8.1 and 8.3 suggest that isometric projections of three-dimensional space are, in fact, easier to understand than third-angle projections. The difference between the mean values of tests R1 and R3 varies by nearly 30 per cent.

The bar charts presented in these figures, however, do not reveal whether the difference between the results is *statistically* significant. The Wilcoxon Matched-Pairs Signed-Ranks Test is an appropriate non-parametric statistical test which was designed to assess the significance of difference between two related samples where neither is assumed to have a normal distribution.

9.2.1 The Wilcoxon Matched-Pairs Signed-Ranks Test for H1

Although the data resulting from tests R1 and R3 are on the interval scale, the requirement of Hypothesis 1 (H1) is only that one form of projection is easier to understand than the other. In this case, the data can be considered at the ordinal level where they are ranked. The Wilcoxon Test is more useful than other ranked tests as it accounts for the magnitude as well as the direction of the differences.

9.2.2 The hypothesis and null hypothesis for H1

Hypothesis ($H1_1$) presented in Section 6.3 states that 'isometric projections of three-dimensional space are easier to understand than third-angle projections'.

The null hypothesis for $H1_1$ is $H1_0$. This is the hypothesis of *no* difference which assumes that it is neither easier nor more difficult to understand isometric projections of three-dimensional space than it is to understand third-angle projections.

The null hypothesis was formulated for the purpose of being rejected on the grounds that, if rejected, the alternative hypothesis (H1₁) could be accepted.

If the probability (p) of the difference between the test results were due to a chance sampling error greater than 0.01* (p>0.01), then the null hypothesis would *not* have been rejected. As Table 9.1 below demonstrates, however, the probability of the test being due to sampling error was, in fact, less than 0.01 (p<0.01). The null hypothesis was therefore rejected, and the hypothesis accepted, leading to the conclusion that the sample groups collectively found the isometric projections to be significantly easier to understand than the third-angle projections.

Table 9.1. The Wilcoxon Signed-Ranks Test: Results for R1 and R3

Ranks		N	Mean rank	Sum of ranks
R3 - R1	Negative Ranks	81 [a]	50.22	4067.50
	Positive Ranks	10 [b]	11.85	118.50
	Ties	6 [c]		
	Total	97		

Test statistics	R3 - R1
Z	-7.824
Exact significance ** (1-tailed) ***	0.000

[a] R3 < R1   [b] R3 > R1   [c] R1 = R3   Z = Standard score

* It is common practice in social science studies to accept the 0.05 or the 0.01 level of significance. The 0.01 level of significance was chosen as it reduces the risk of a committing a Type I error: i.e. the chance of rejecting the null hypothesis when in fact it is true. Setting a level of significance to an even more rigorous

standard would run the risk of committing a Type II error: i.e. not rejecting the null hypothesis when in fact it should be rejected.

** Exact tests were used as they provide a means for obtaining accurate results when data fail to meet any of the underlying assumptions necessary for reliable results using the standard asymptotic method: i.e. they are useful when the data set is small, sparse, contains many ties, is unbalanced, or is poorly distributed. Asymptotic results obtained from small data sets or sparse or unbalanced tables can be misleading as the asymptotic method assumes that the data set is reasonably large, and that tables are densely populated and well balanced (Cohen and Holliday, 1984).

*** As the hypothesis predicted the *direction* in which the difference was to lie, a 'one-tailed' test was performed.

9.2.3 Additional analyses relating to H1

Although the analysis above demonstrates that collectively the sample groups found the isometric projections to be significantly easier to understand than the third-angle projections, it does not show whether this was the case for individual groups. Bar chart (a) presented in Figure 9.1: p.151, however, does reveal that every group found the isometric projections easier to understand, but that the *difference* in understanding between the two types was greater for WEDC postgraduate students than for any of the other groups. A comparison of Tests R5 with R6 (presented in Table 9.2) although performed by only one of the subject groups (WEDC postgraduates), nevertheless corroborated the results of the comparison of Tests R1 and R3.

144

Table 9.2. The Wilcoxon Signed-Ranks Test: Results for R5 and R6

Ranks		No.	Mean Rank	Sum of Ranks
R6 - R5	Negative Ranks	16 [a]	8.50	136.00
	Positive Ranks	0 [b]	0	0.00
	Ties	0 [c]		
	Total	16		

Test statistics	R5 - R6
Z	-3.526
Exact significance ** (1-tailed) ***	0.000

[a] R6 < R5   [b] R6 > R5   [c] R5 = R6   Z = Standard score

9.2.4 Selected variables and categories

Section 8.3 gave reasons for selecting variables and categories for further analysis. These are presented in Table 9.3 below, first by *Subject group* and then alphabetically.

Figure 9.1(b) - 9.1(l): pp. 151-6 presents the differences between the mean scores of R1 and R3 for the other key variables as listed in Table 9.3. It can be seen from these figures that the mean results of the scores were greater for R1 than R3 in every case.

9.2.5 Test R2

The requirement of Test R2 to represent the plan view of objects demanded of the subject skills in both interpreting the three-dimensional objects pictures on Task Sheet R2 *and* in representing the object orthographically. As the requirement of this test differs from the requirements of R1, R3, R5 and R6 (which only demands skills in interpreting either one or other of the projections), it has not been considered in the above analyses. The test was designed, however, to establish whether subjects found it difficult to connect the three-dimensional skills required to interpret the pictures with the orthographic skills required to represent a single plane view of the objects. The mean average of the test results given in Table 8.17 closely match those for Tests R1 and R5 (the isometric projection tests) and not those for R3 and R6 (the third-angle projection tests). This suggests in this instance that the perceptual skills of interpreting isometric projections are more predominant than the perceptual skills of third-angle projection, although both are necessary to complete the task.

Table 9.3. Selected variables and categories

Variable	Categories
Subject group	WEDC postgraduate students Civil Engineering postgraduate students Civil Engineering undergraduate students LUSAD pre-degree students NUST Civil Engineering undergraduate students
Age	15-20 21-30 31 and over *
Artistic background	No Yes
Educational level	Pre-degree Undergraduate Postgraduate
English as first language	No Yes
Ethnic origin	African European
Formal training in engineering drawing	No Yes
Gender	Male Female
Handedness	Left-handed Right-handed
Professional status	Engineer (includes architect/planner/surveyor) * Non-technologist (includes scientist) *
Region (economic)	High-income country Low-income country
Work experience	Less than 5 years Over 5 years *

Clustered categories are marked *

146

9.3. Comparative analyses of variables and categories (H2)

The analyses presented in Section 9.2 reveal the differences between the results of R1 and R3 and lead to an acceptance of the first hypothesis (H1$_1$) assuming a chance sampling error less than 0.01. The second hypothesis (H2$_1$) states that 'the ability of adult learners to understand the pictorial conventions of isometric projection and third-angle projection is significantly affected by one or more of the variables listed in Section 6.3.'

The null hypotheses for H2$_1$ is H2$_0$ which, by contrast, assumes that 'the ability of adult learners to understand the pictorial conventions of isometric projection and third-angle projection is *not* significantly affected by one or more of the variables listed in Section 6.3.' Again, if the probability (p) of the difference between the test results were due to a chance sampling error greater than 0.01 (p>0.01), then the null hypotheses would *not* be rejected. Analysis of the results of Tests R1 and R5 (for isometric projection) and R3 and R6 (for third-angle projection) reveals whether or not this is the case for one or more of the variables, leading to the acceptance or rejection of the hypothesis for both types of projection.

9.3.1 Comparison of means

Bar charts presenting a comparison of the mean scores between categories within each variable illustrate the differences between the results (Figure 9.2 to 9.5: pp.157-164).

It is clear from these bar charts that the mean scores for categories within most variables are similar. To establish whether there is any association between the scores and the variables for any of the four tests, it was first of all necessary to grade the scores. Grading produced discrete categories enabling the data to be analysed at the ordinal level using the Pearson Chi-square test and, in some cases, the Fisher Exact test. Grading was necessary here as the data did not fulfil the criteria for the (parametric) ANOVA test for the comparison of means.

The grading system used was:

0-20	Very low
21-40	Low
41-60	Medium
61-80	High
81-100	Very high

Another way of expressing Hypothesis 2 is to suggest that the scores of the tests are dependent on one or other of the key variables. By comparing expected and observed frequencies of the levels of response (Very low - Very high) for each variable using the chi-square test, it is possible to determine whether the scores are, in fact, dependent on any of the variables: i.e. if the observed and expected frequencies are significantly different, then the variable would be seen to have influenced the results.

Chi-square tests were performed for each of the four tests (R1, R3, R5 and R6) for every key variable. Fisher exact tests were also performed where possible: i.e. where variables only comprised two categories.

Table 9.4 presents the exact significance levels of the tests being due to chance sampling error, based on chi-square cross tabulation calculations. The Fisher Exact results are not presented here as in no case did they differ sufficiently from the exact chi-square results to influence inferences that may be drawn: i.e. the Fisher results did not fall on opposing sides of the 0.05 or 0.01 probability thresholds calculated using the chi-square test.

Table 9.4. Pearson Chi-square cross tabulation calculations for R1, R3, R5 and R6

Selected variables	Isometric projection tests		Third-angle projection tests	
	R1	R5	R3	R6
Subject group	0.351	*	0.249	*
Age	0.531	0.174	0.398	0.222
Artistic background	0.360	*	0.681	*
Educational level	0.826	*	0.266	*
English as first language	**0.003**	0.432	0.226	0.120
Ethnic origin	**0.045**	**0.040**	0.311	0.155
Formal training in ed.	0.225	0.238	0.989	0.652
Gender	0.951	0.087	**0.031**	0.924
Handedness	0.452	0.653	0.822	0.924
Professional status	0.951	0.657	0.691	0.677
Region (economic)	0.160	**0.046**	0.126	0.113
Work experience	0.269	0.093	0.069	0.558

* Values not computed as variables were constant.

It can be seen from the table above that in all but five instances (shown in bold type) the chance sampling error was greater than 0.05 ($p > 0.05$) and that in all but one instance (shown in the shaded cell) the chance sampling error was greater than 0.01 ($p > 0.01$). In other words, the null hypothesis ($H2_0$) cannot be rejected except in these instances and only in the case of *English as first language*, if the same chance sampling error for Hypothesis 2 ($H2_1$) as for Hypothesis 1 ($H1_1$) is assumed.

9.4. Comparative analyses of variables and categories (H3)

This section analyses the data collected for Test R4. This test was designed to assess whether recognition of the laws of linear perspective as a primary means of understanding pictorial space is significantly affected by one or more of the listed variables. It should be emphasized that this test (unlike the other tests) is only concerned with *preferred methods of pictorial perception* and not with ability.

Unlike data collected for the other tests, Test R4 data are nominal. They are also less reliable, given the experimental nature of the test design described in Section 7.4.6. In other words, reliability of the test design is a major assumption in accepting or rejecting Hypothesis 3 (H3$_1$) based on the data collected for Test R4.

The data collected for Test R4 is grouped so that results are recorded as either containing or not containing A. Where A is recorded, the subject has demonstrated that he or she recognizes the laws of linear perspective as a primary means of defining pictorial space. Similarly, where A is not recorded the subject has not demonstrated this.

The bar charts presented from cross-tabulations for each variable reveal that there are, in fact, differences (see Figure 9.6: pp.165-6). The significance of these differences was computed using chi-square tests as described above. The results are presented in Table 9.5.

Table 9.5. Pearson Chi-square cross tabulation calculations for R4

Selected variables	R4
Subject group	**0.007**
Age	**0.002**
Artistic background	**0.001**
Educational level	**0.001**
English as first language	**0.000**
Ethnic origin	**0.000**
Formal training in ed.	0.282
Gender	0.542
Handedness	1.000
Professional status	**0.038**
Region (economic)	**0.000**
Work experience	**0.001**

Given the experimental nature of Test R4, Hypothesis (H3) can be neither accepted nor rejected as a result of this analysis. These data suggest, however, that a number of variables influence the ways in which subjects interpret pictorial space.

Figure 9.1 Comparison of the mean values of R1 and R3 for selected variables

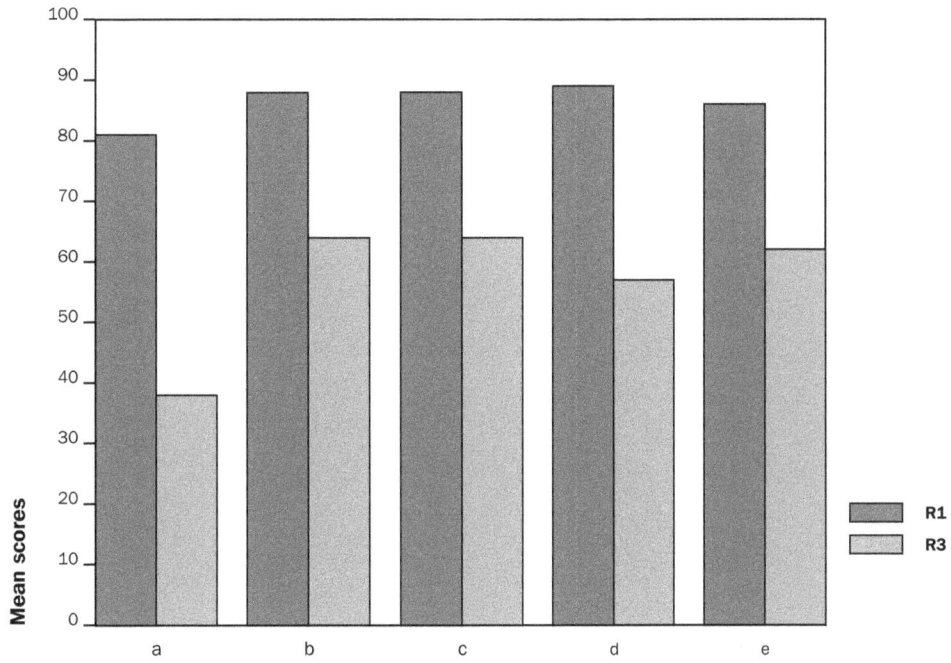

9.1a Subject group

a) WEDC postgraduate students
b) Civil Engineering postgraduate students (Loughborough)
c) Civil Engineering undergraduate students (Loughborough)
d) Loughborough University School of Art and Design pre-degree students
e) NUST Civil Engineering undergraduate students (Bulawayo)

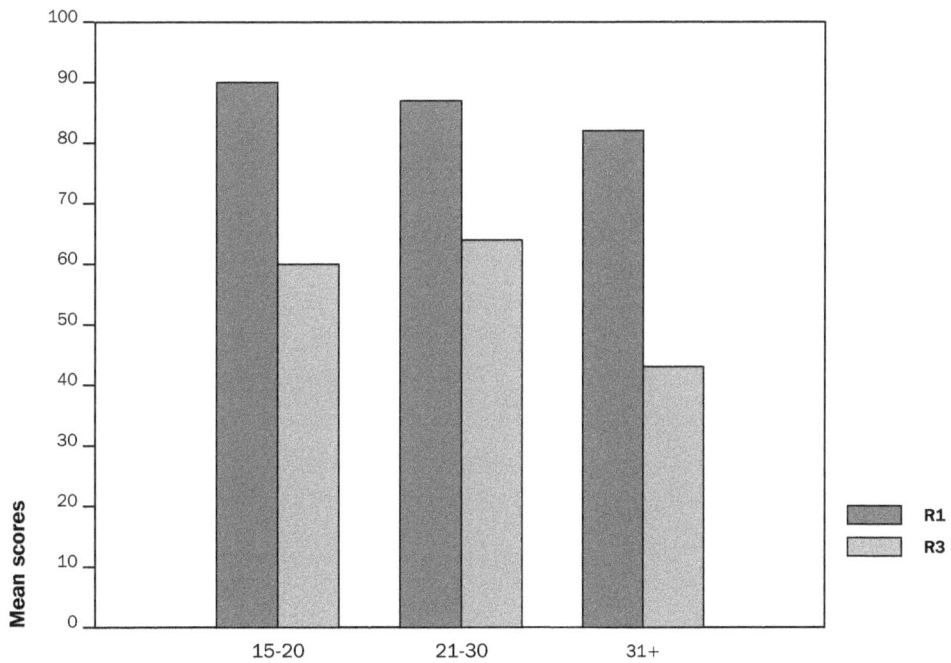

9.1b Age

Figure 9.1   (continued)

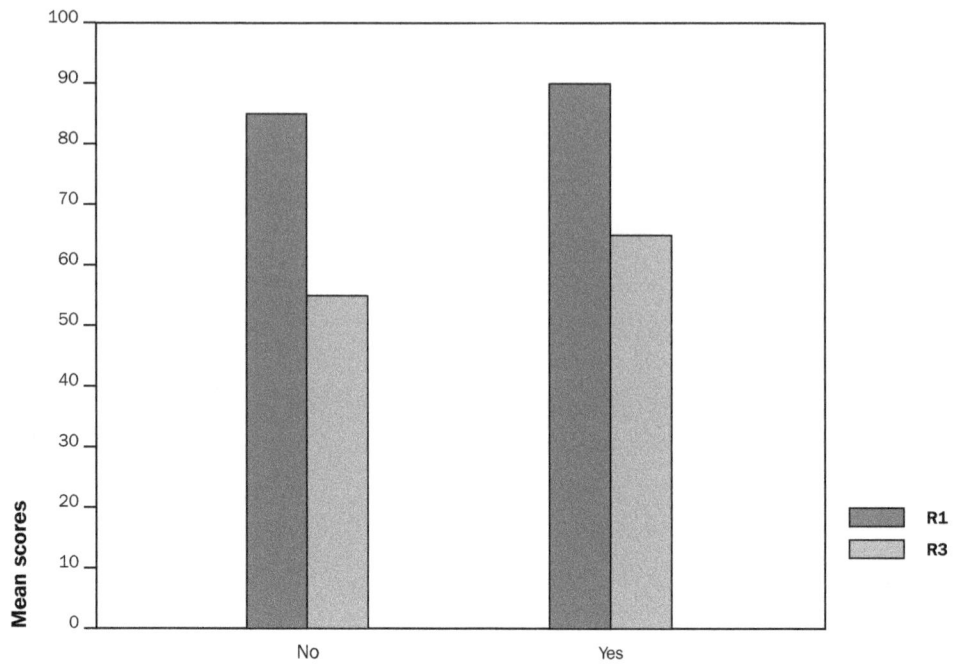

9.1c Artistic background

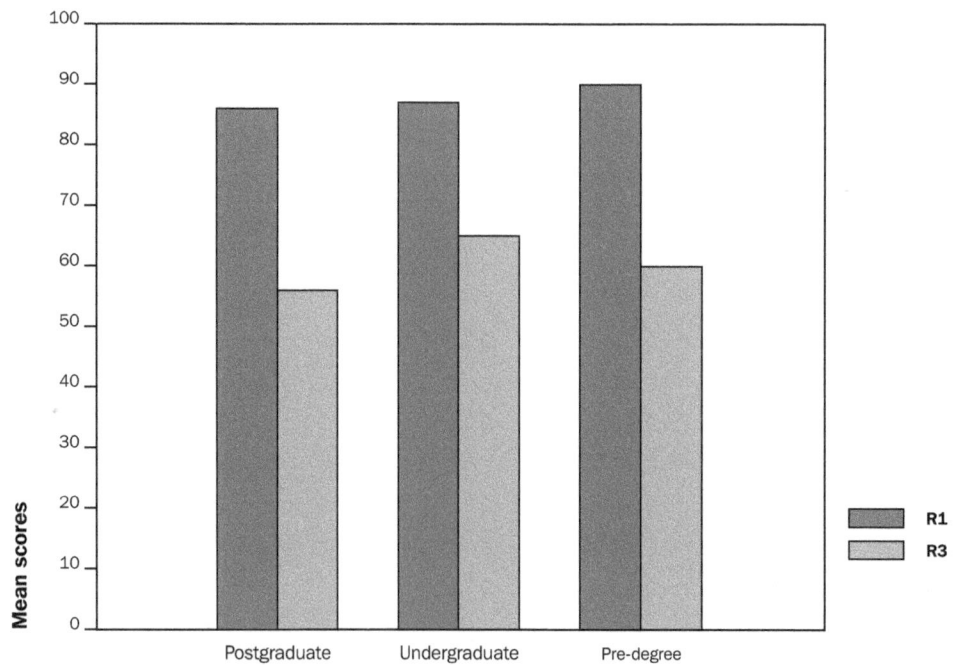

9.1d Educational level

Figure 9.1 (continued)

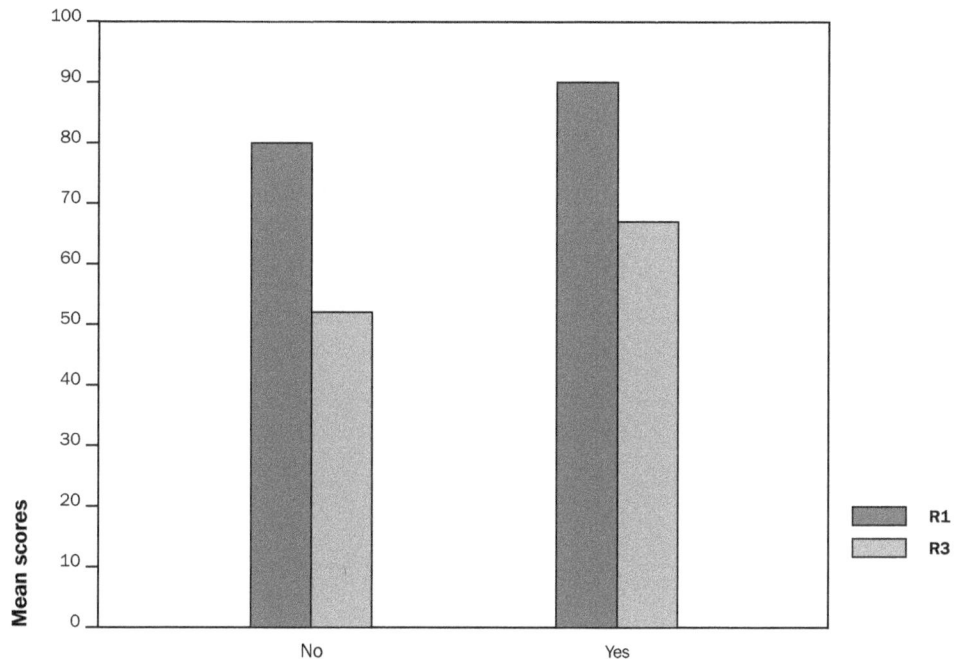

9.1e English is first language

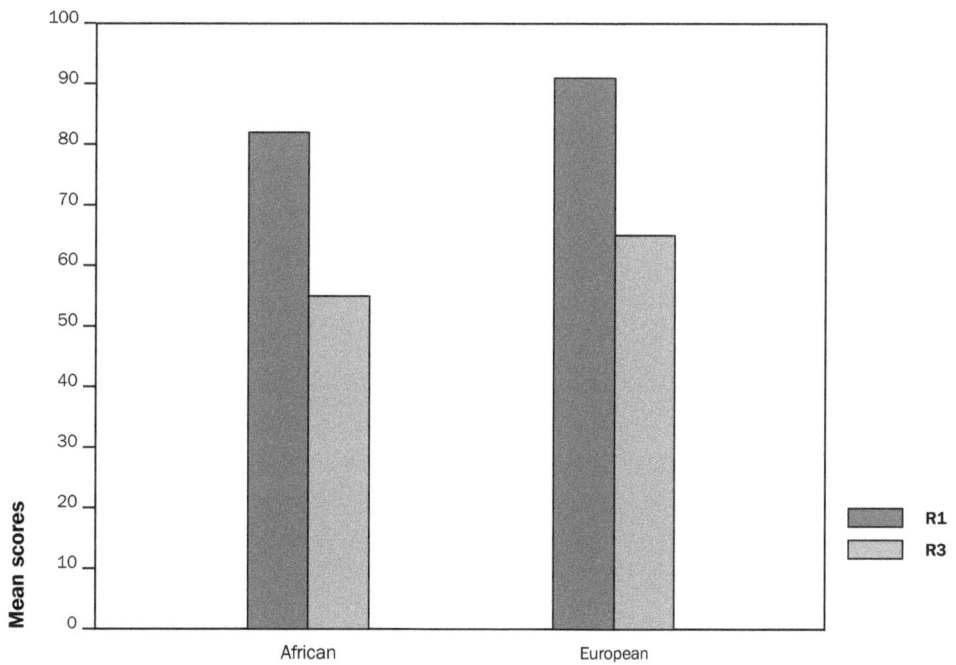

9.1f Ethnic origin (African or European)

Figure 9.1 **(continued)**

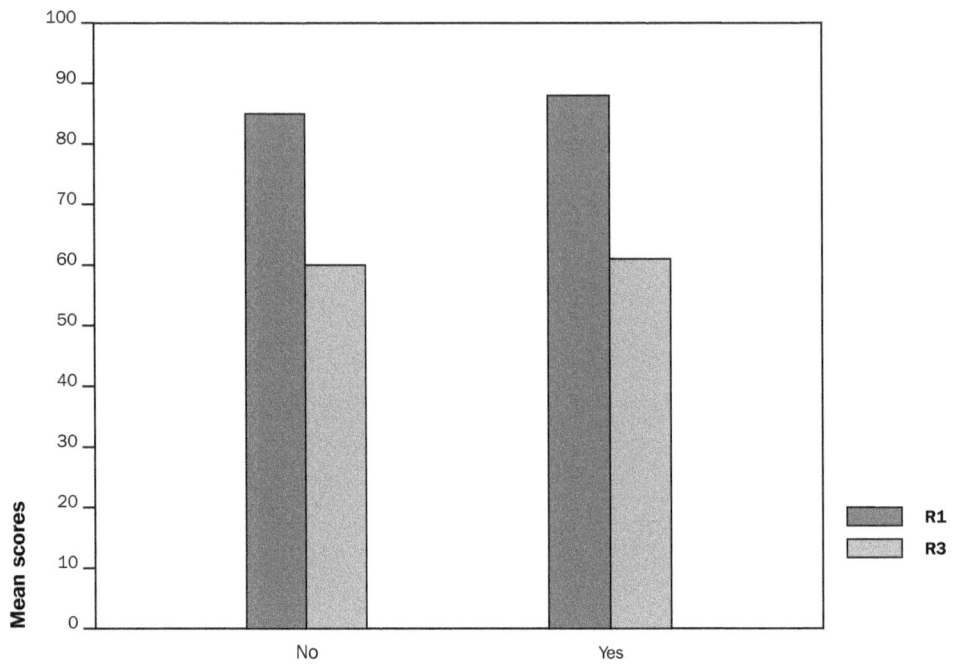

9.1g Formal training in engineering drawing or technical illustration

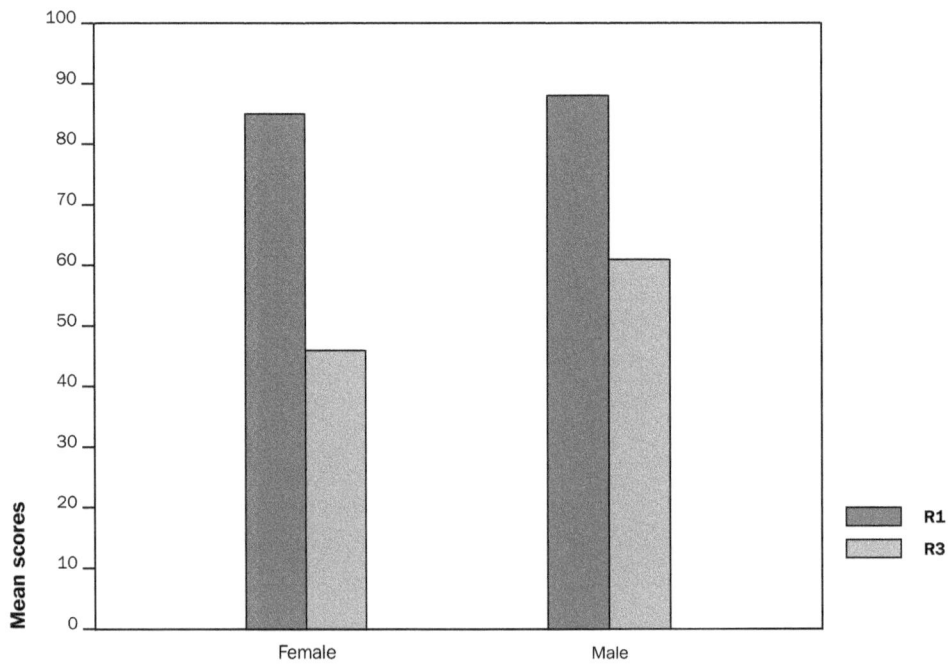

9.1h Gender

154

Figure 9.1 (continued)

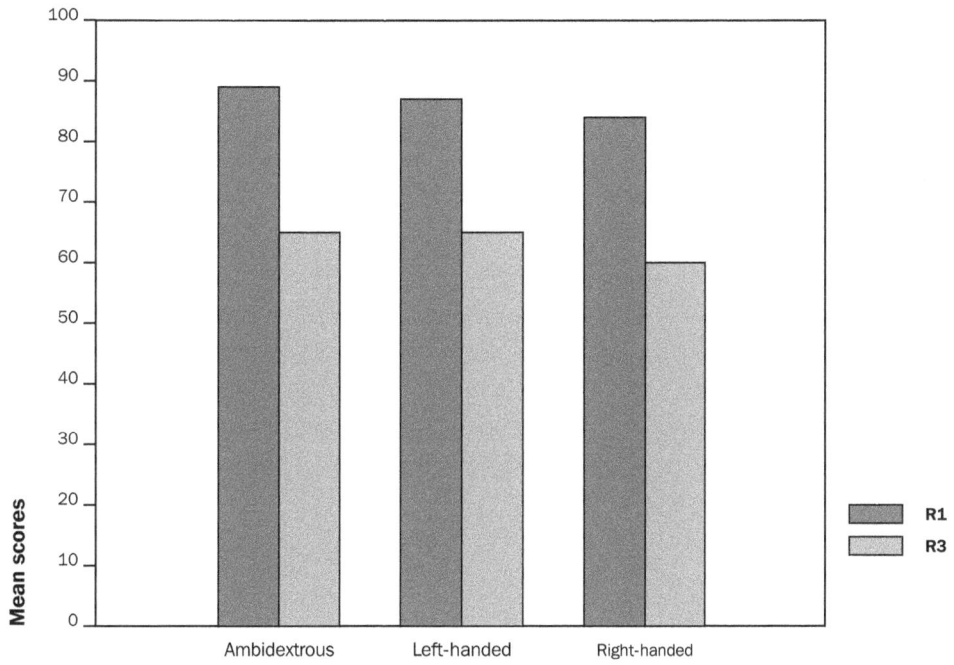

9.1i Handedness

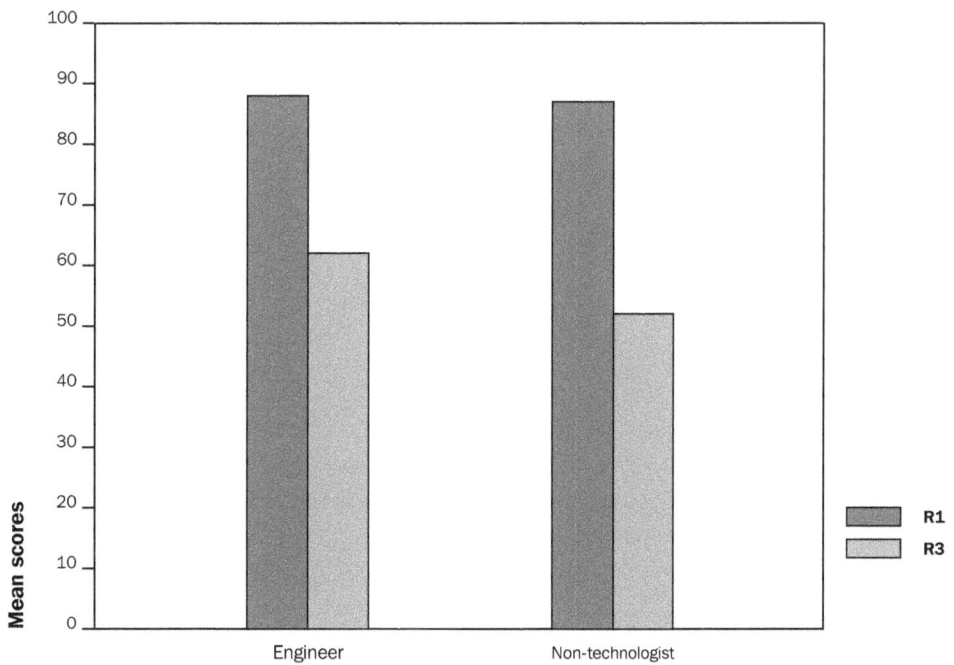

9.1j Professional status

155

Figure 9.1   (continued)

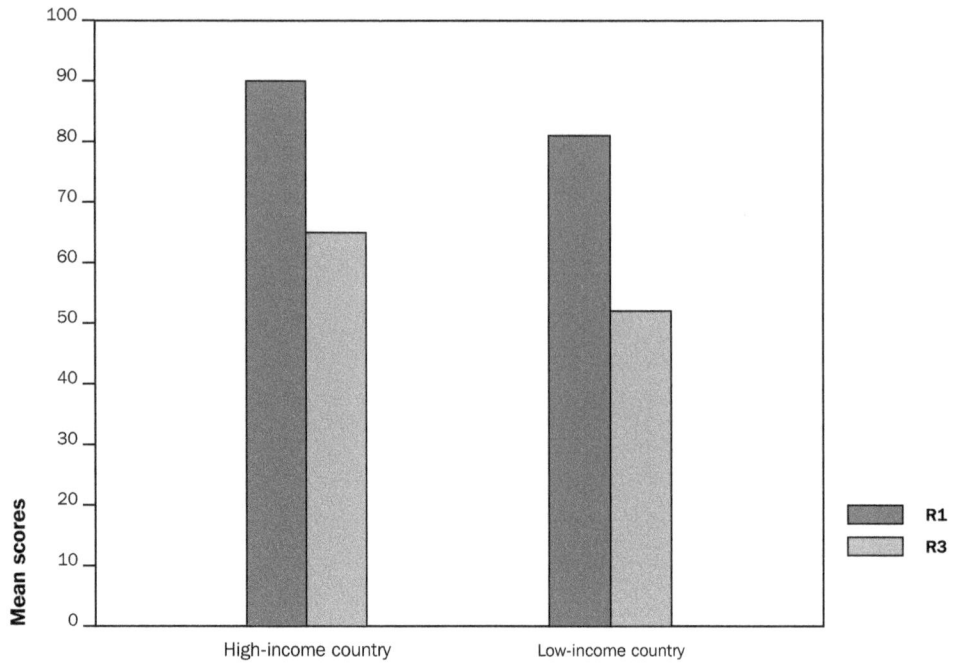

9.1k Region

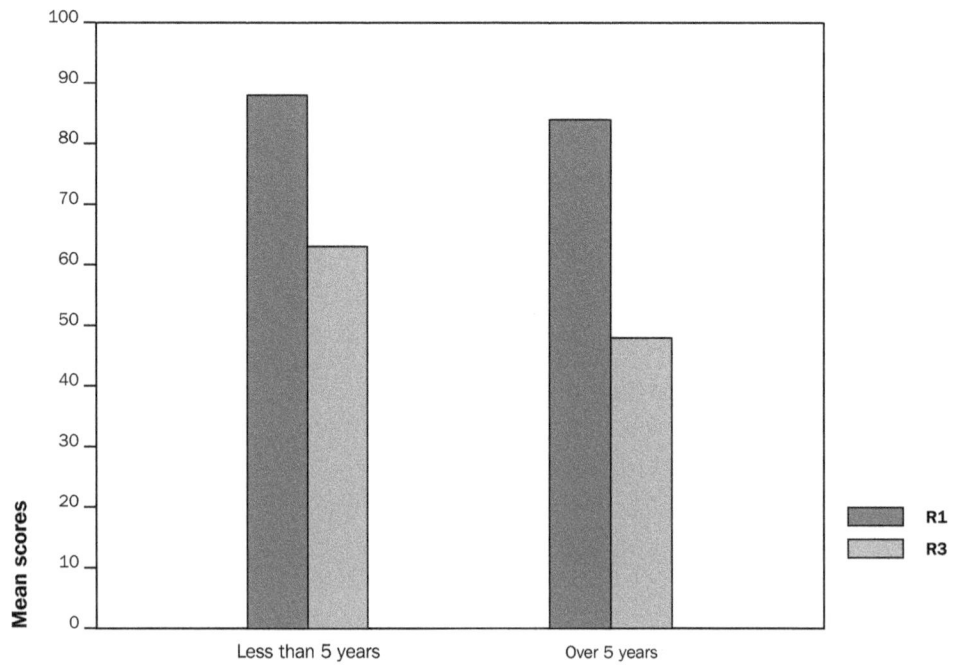

9.1l Work experience

**Figure 9.2 Comparison of means by selected variable for the results of Test R1
(Isometric drawing completion task)**

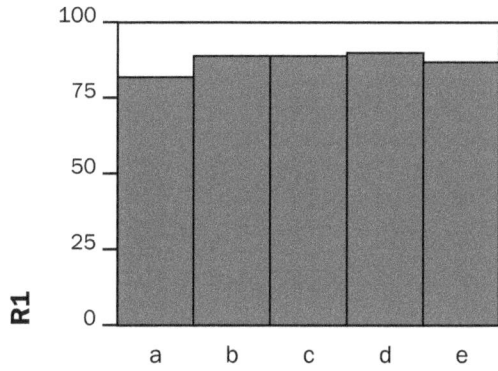

9.2a Subject group

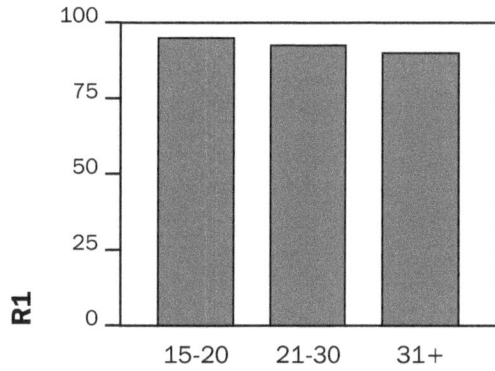

9.2b Age

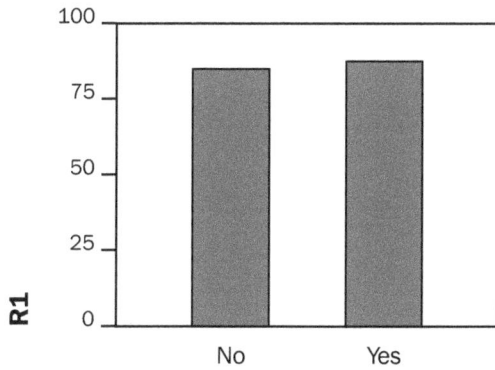

9.2c Artistic background

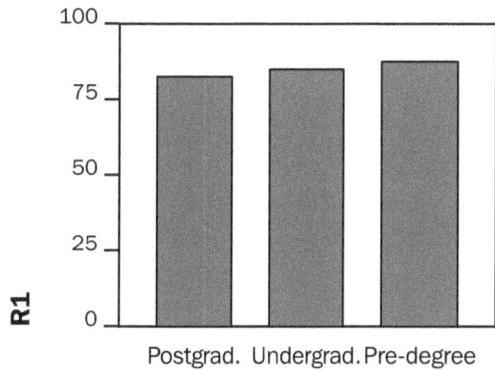

9.2d Educational level

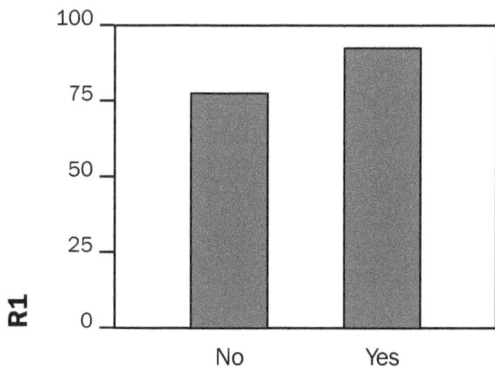

9.2e English is first language

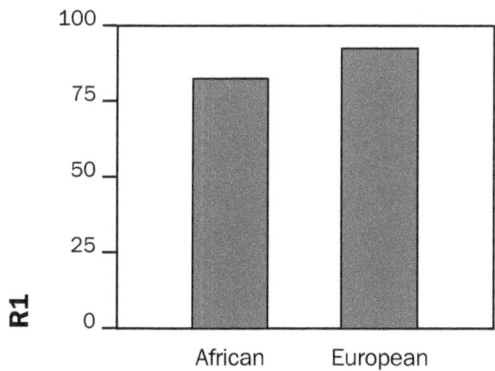

9.2f Ethnic origin

Figure 9.2   (continued)

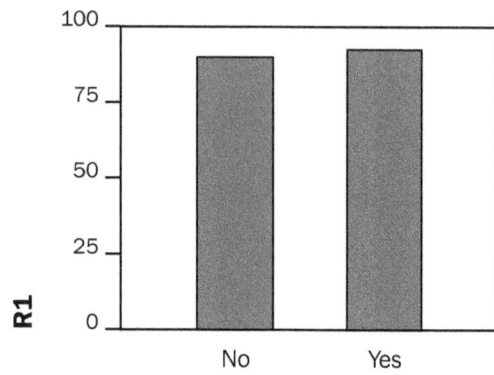

9.2g Formal training

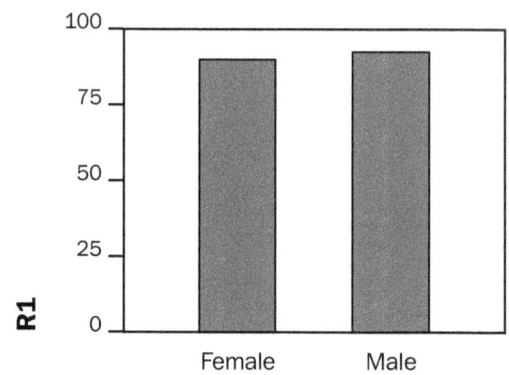

9.2h Gender

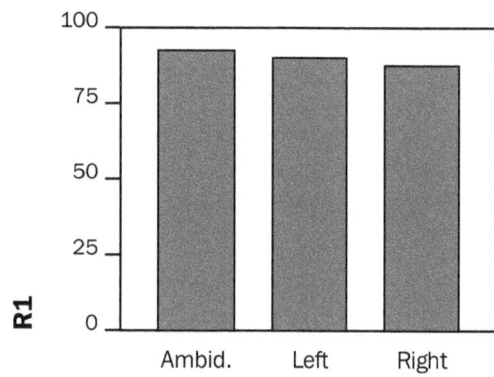

9.2i Handedness

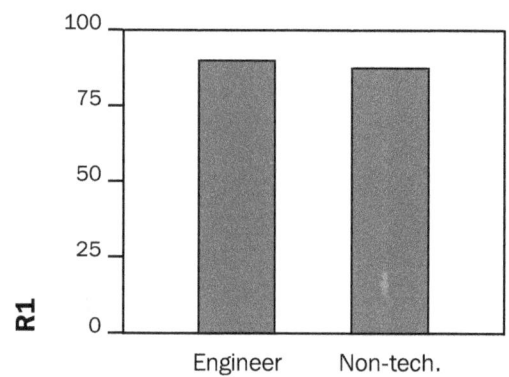

9.2j Professional status

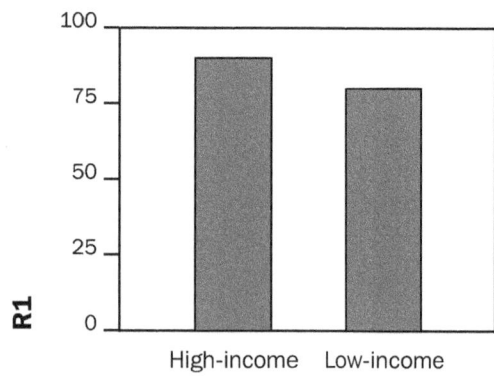

9.2k Region

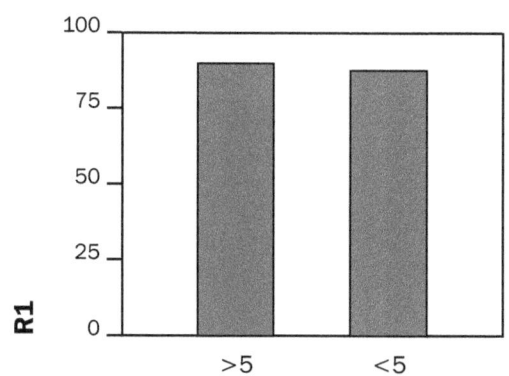

9.2l Work experience

Figure 9.3 Comparison of means by selected variable for the results of Test R3 (Third-angle projection drawing completion task)

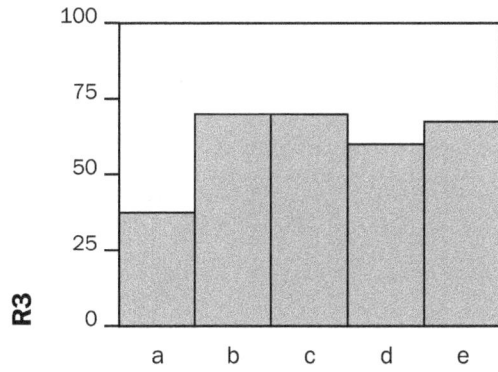

9.3a Subject group

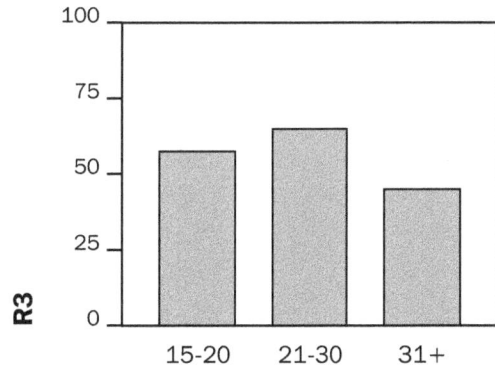

9.3b Age

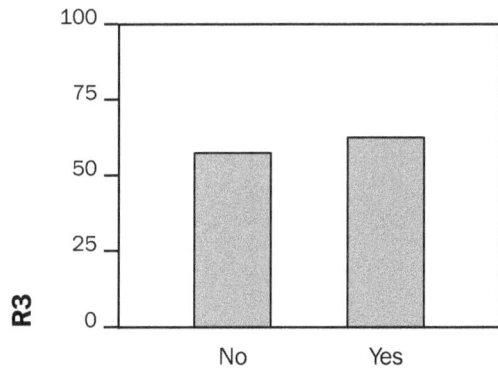

9.3c Artistic background

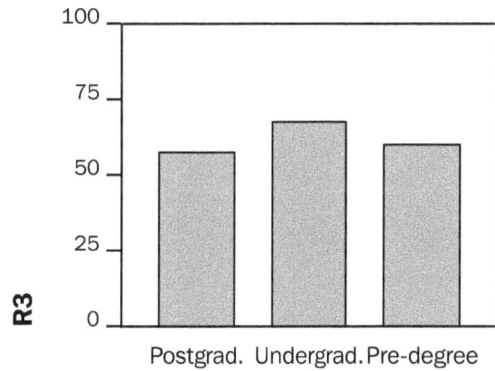

9.3d Educational level

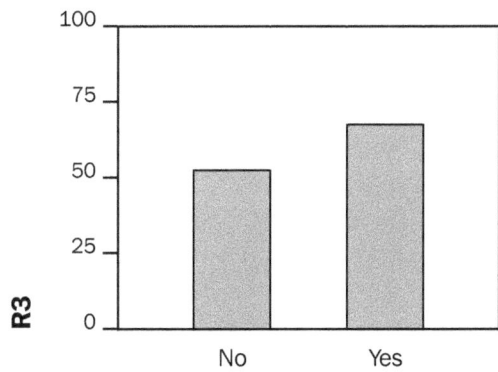

9.3e English is first language

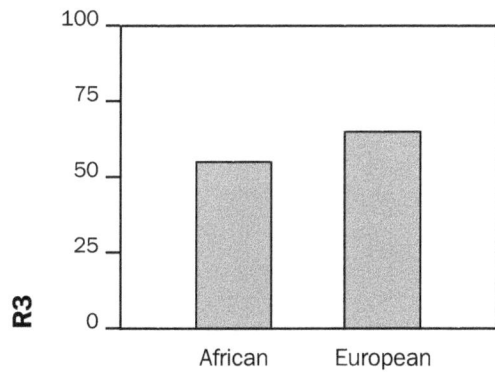

9.3f Ethnic origin

159

Figure 9.3   (continued)

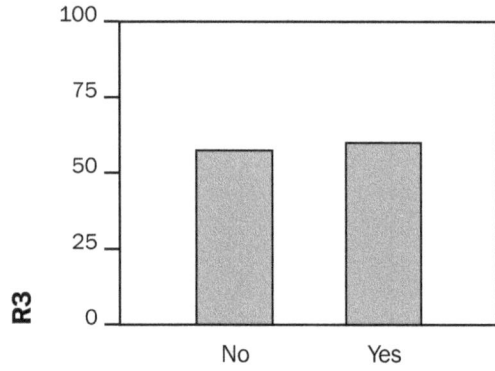

9.3g Formal training

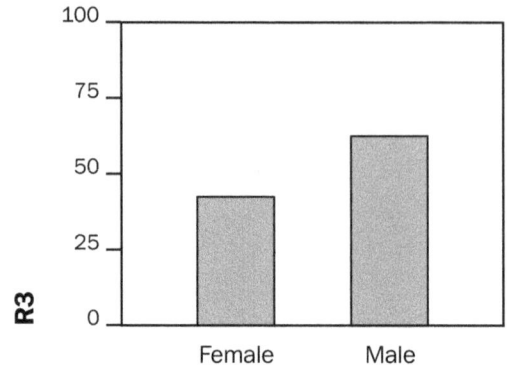

9.3h Gender

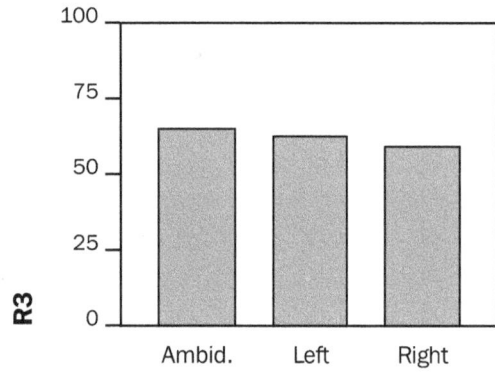

9.3i Handedness

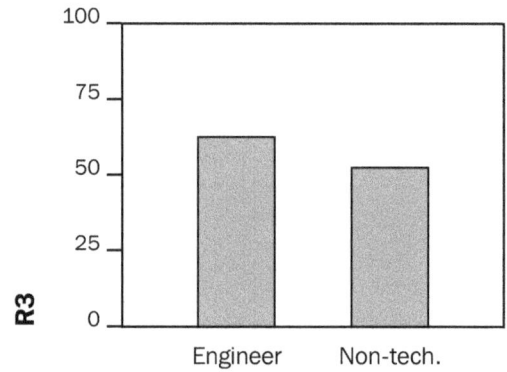

9.3j Professional status

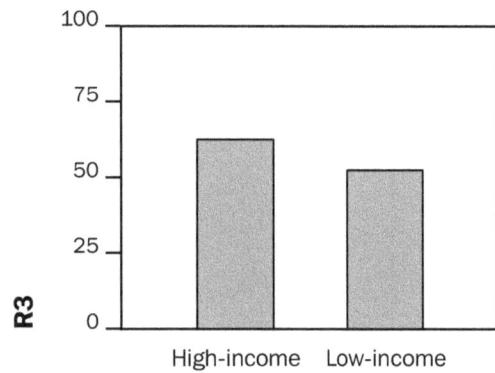

9.3k Region

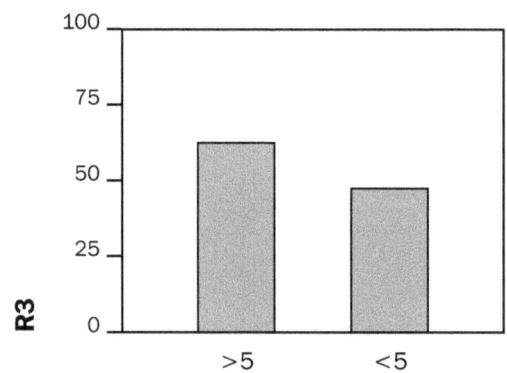

9.3l Work experience

Figure 9.4   Comparison of means by selected variable for the results of Test R5 (Isometric construction task)

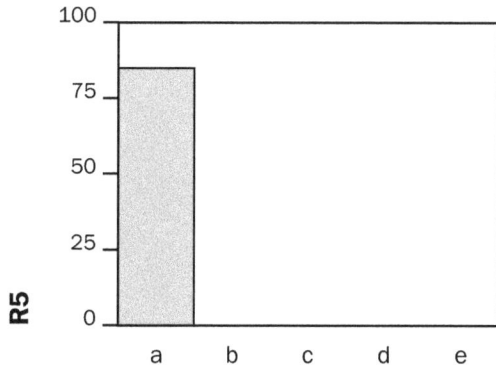

9.4a Subject group

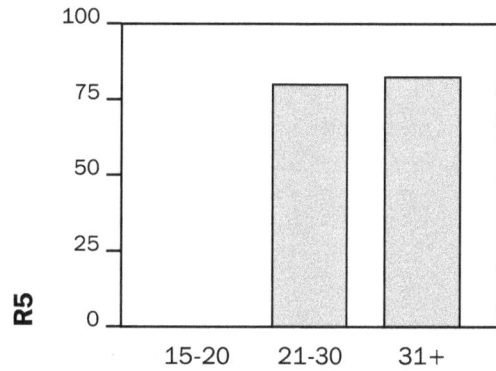

9.4b Age

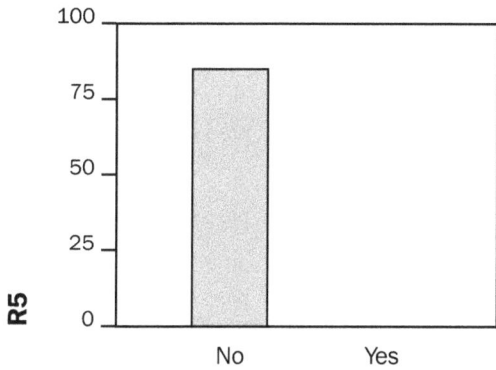

9.4c Artistic background

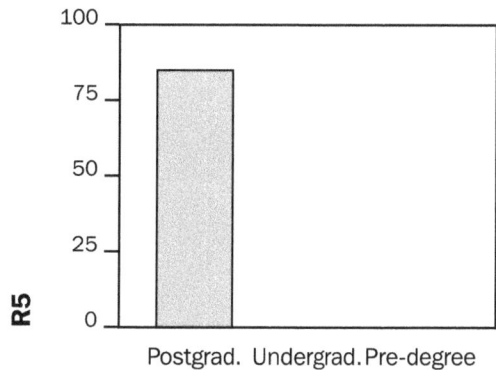

9.4d Educational level

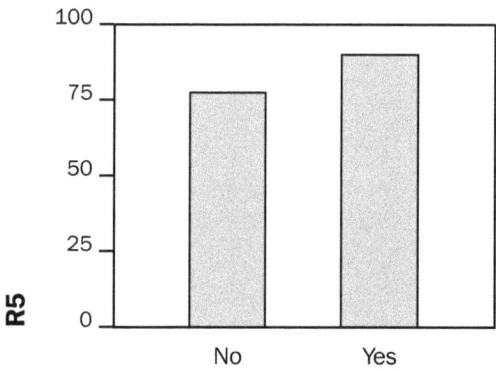

9.4e English is first language

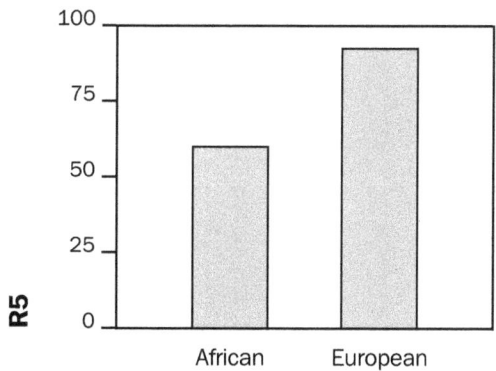

9.4f Ethnic origin

Figure 9.4   (continued)

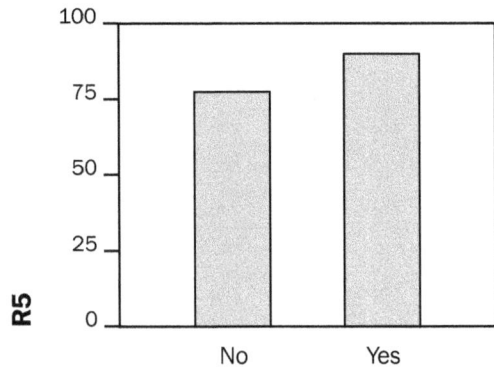

9.4g Formal training

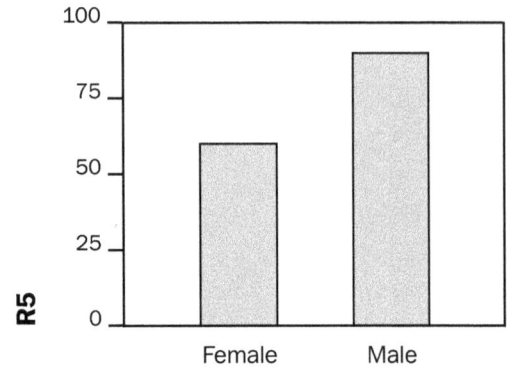

9.4h Gender

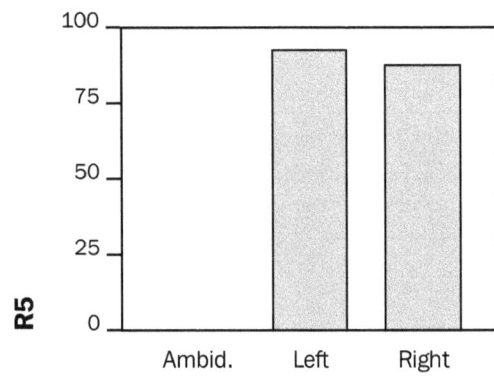

9.4i Handedness

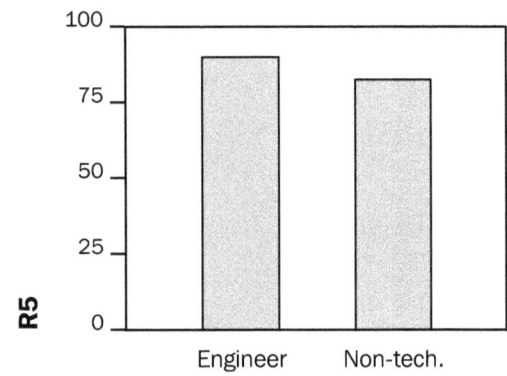

9.4j Professional status

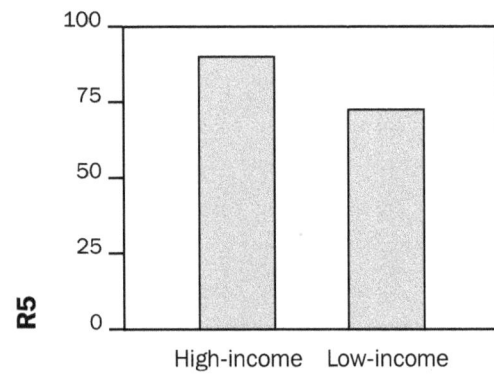

9.4k Region

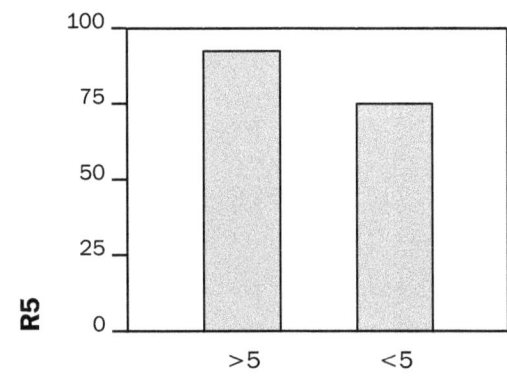

9.4l Work experience

162

Figure 9.5   Comparison of means by selected variable for the results of Test R6 (Third-angle projection construction task)

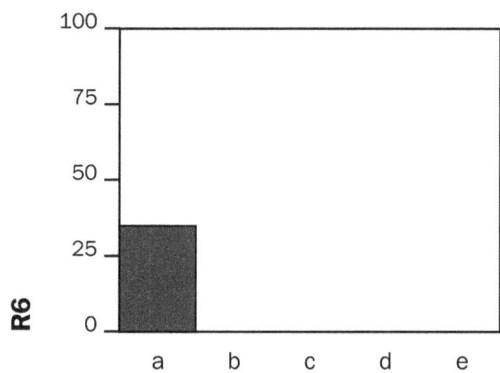

9.5a Subject group

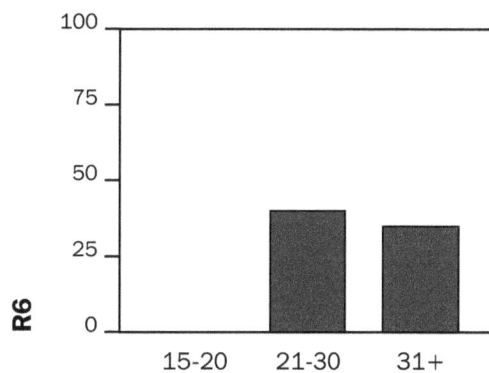

9.5b Age

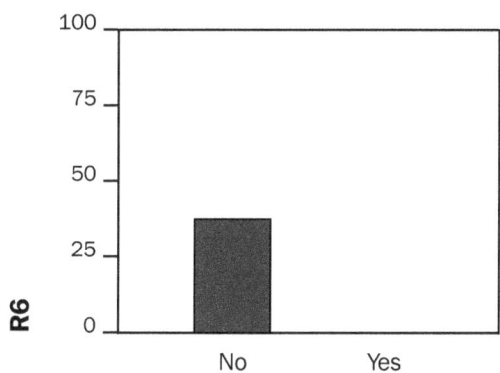

9.5c Artistic background

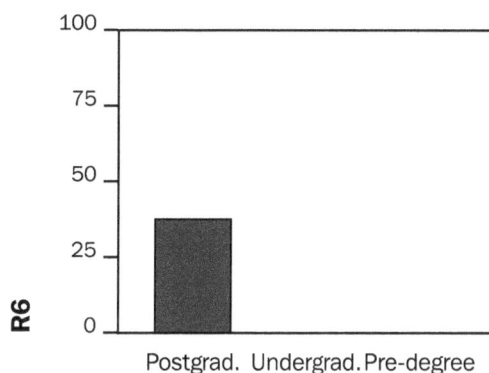

9.5d Educational level

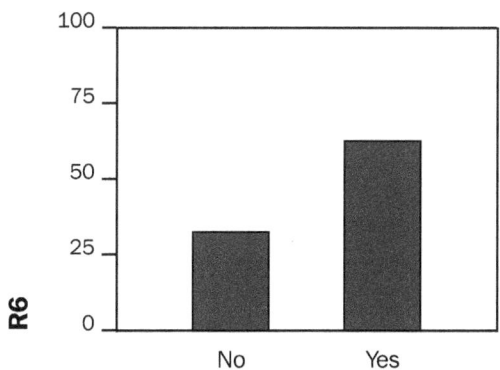

9.5e English is first language

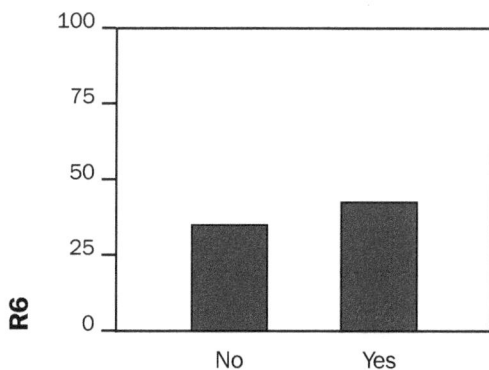

9.5g Formal training

Figure 9.5   (continued)

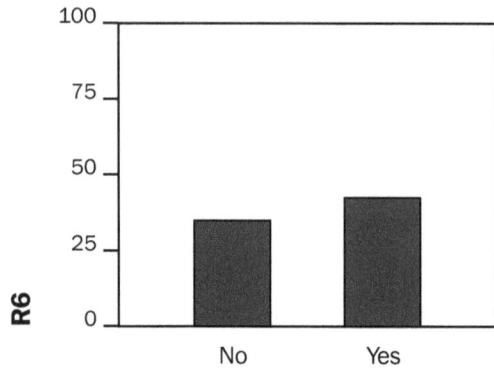

9.5g Formal training

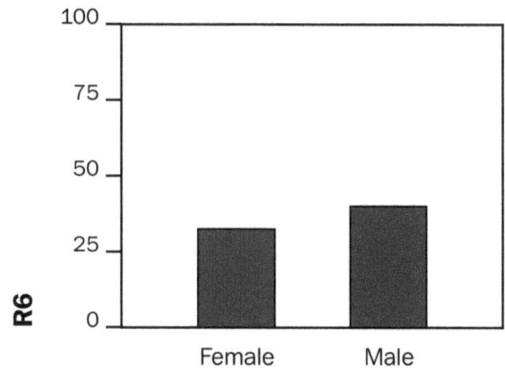

9.5h Gender

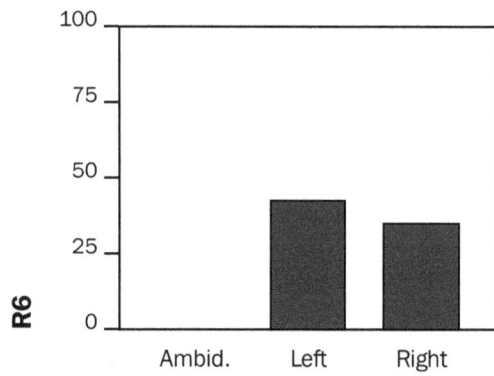

9.5i Handedness

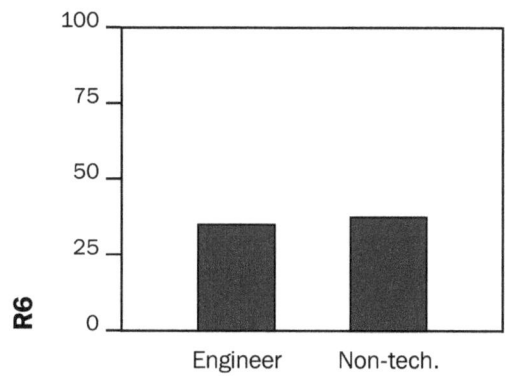

9.5j Professional status

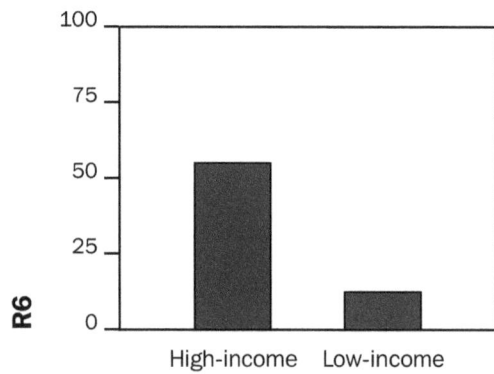

9.5k Region

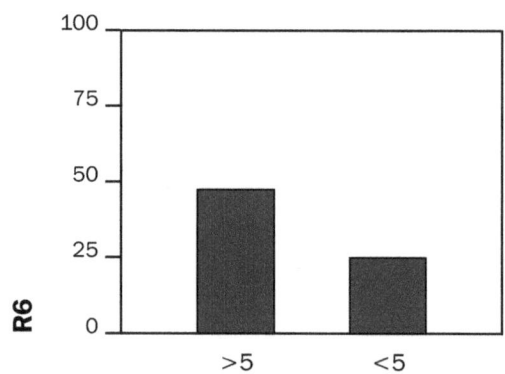

9.5l Work experience

164

Figure 9.6 Crosstabulation results for R4

Where A is recorded, the subject has demonstrated that he or she recognizes the laws of linear perspective as a primary means of defining pictorial space. Where A is not recorded, the subject has not demonstrated this.

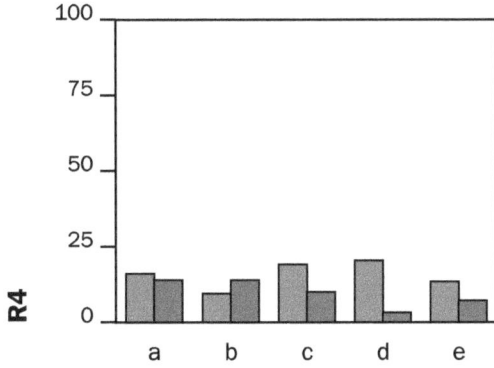

9.6a Subject group

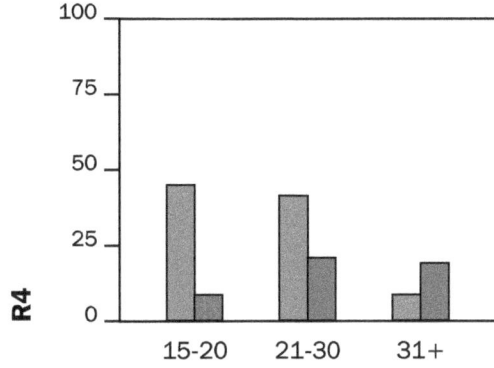

9.6b Age

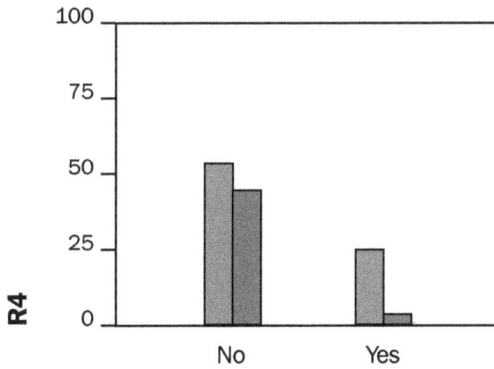

9.6c Artistic background

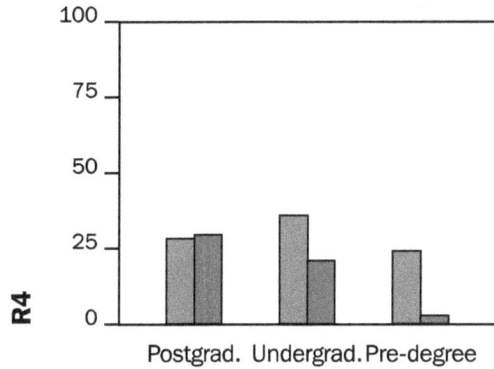

9.6d Educational level

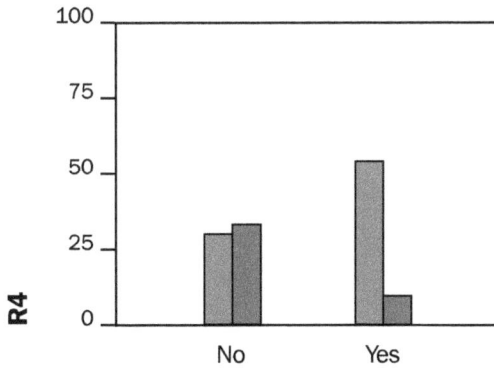

9.6e English is first language

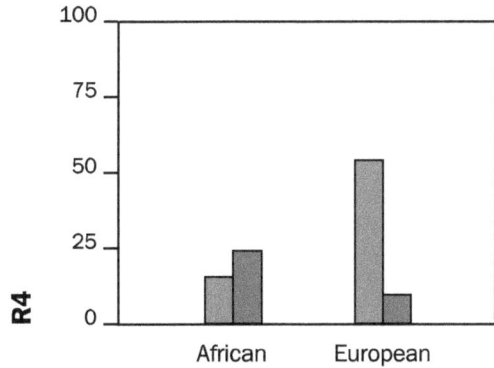

9.6f Ethnic origin

Figure 9.6   (continued)

Legend:
- ▨ Contains A
- ▨ Does not contain A

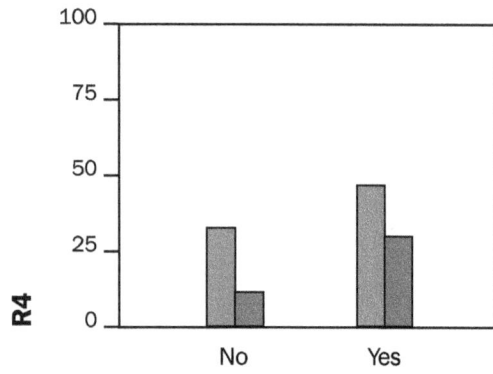

9.6g Formal training

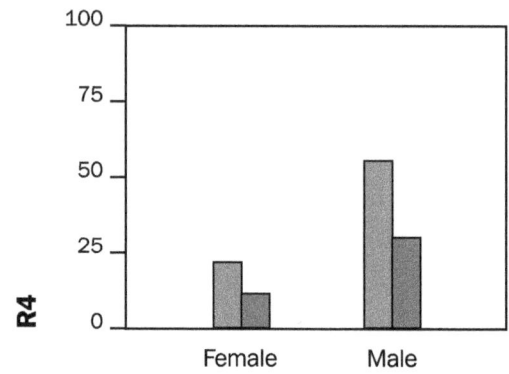

9.6h Gender

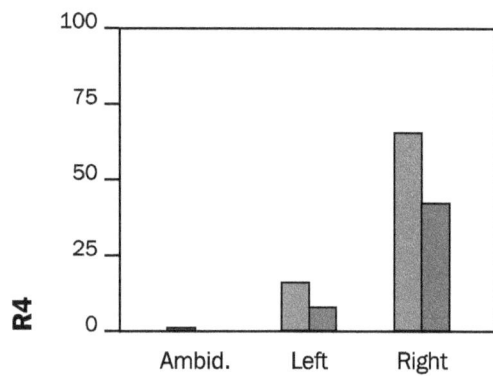

9.6i Handedness

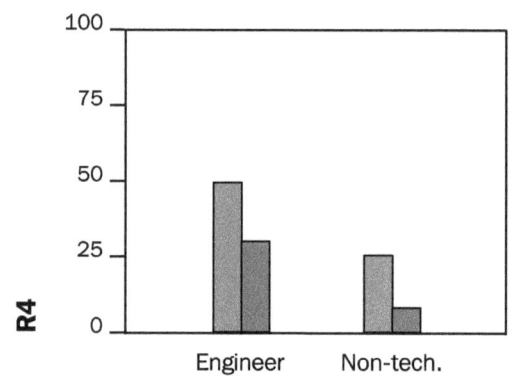

9.6j Professional status

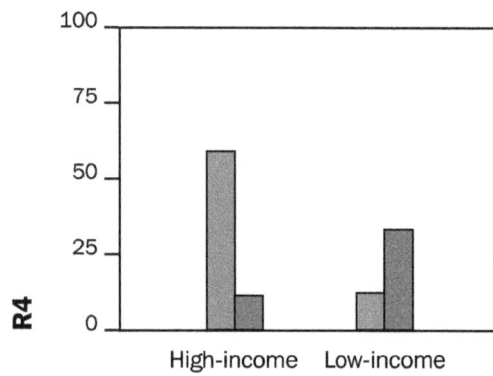

9.6k Region

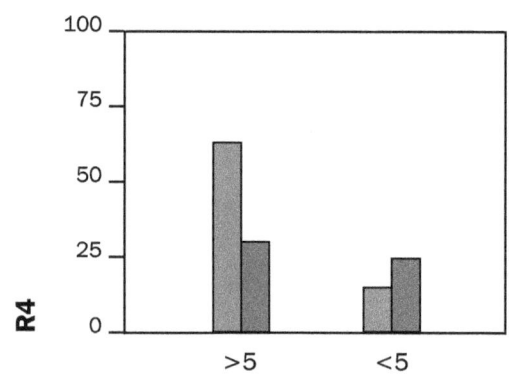

9.6l Work experience

PART III

Chapter 10

Conclusions

10.1. Introduction

This chapter presents the conclusions drawn from both the literature review presented in Part I and the research results and analysis presented in Part II. It also identifies areas for further study.

10.2. Conclusions drawn from the literature review

10.2.1 Learning and adult education

It is clear from the literature concerning learning and adult education that there is little agreement among authors about what learning actually is, but that there is much agreement that learning leads to positive changes in attitudes, performance or behaviour.

People go about learning in different ways which range from the re-inforcement of behaviour through practice, to learning by insight based on the re-interpretation of existing knowledge in the light of new experience.

Learning involves the active processing of information from different sources, and is enhanced:

- when learning objectives are clear;

- when there is opportunity for practice;

- when it is rewarded;

- when instruction is well structured and organized, and takes into account the individual differences of learners, their learning styles and their existing knowledge; and

- when it takes place within a supportive and relaxed environment where freedom to experiment or 'play' is encouraged.

Professional people are likely to have had experience of 'learning how to learn' and as a result are also likely to be able to undertake self-directed learning. Collaborative learning may not be as appealing or appropriate to professionals as traditional or self-directed modes of learning.

10.2.2 International development and distance learning

There is a clear need for education and training of professionals working in international development, not least for practitioners involved with the planning, provision and management of physical infrastructure.

Distance learning offers an appropriate, alternative way of learning, especially for the development professional whose circumstances restrict attendance of conventional education and training courses, but who is nevertheless well-motivated and able to apply new learning to existing work situations.

Distance learning is most effective when the methods and technologies used are appropriate to the instructional tasks, and there is student-to-student and student-to-tutor interaction. Performance of students on project work and continuous assessment is generally better for distance learning students than for those on full-time courses. Learners can apply newly-acquired skills to their work as soon as they are gained which enhances both work performance and learning.

Distance learners bring basic characteristics to their learning experience which influence their success in coursework. Such learners are voluntarily seeking further education; have post-secondary education goals with expectations for higher grades; and are highly motivated and self-disciplined.

Learners benefit significantly from a well-designed syllabus. Structured note taking, using tools such as interactive study guides, and the use of visuals and graphics as part of the syllabus, all contribute to understanding.

The key to effective distance education lies in achieving the right balance between the needs of the learners, the requirements of the content, and the constraints faced by the tutor. A strong print component can provide much of the basic instructional content in the form of a course text, as well as readings and other resource material. To a certain extent, the passive nature of print can be offset by systematic instructional design that seeks to stimulate the passive learner. Print has several other advantages. It is spontaneous, instructionally transparent, non-threatening, easy to use, easily reviewed and referenced, easily edited and revised, and is cost- and time-effective.

As print is largely a one-way communication medium, the challenge is to design instruction which maximizes the amount of interaction. The high-level of interactivity between learner and course material, which forms part of the best examples of distance learning, also produces better long-term retention of knowledge and skills.

10.2.3 Information design for self-instruction

All distance learners rely heavily on specially prepared materials: i.e. instruction which is pre-planned and pre-packed. Comprehension is re-inforced by well-structured material which incorporates a range of typographical and design devices from 'chunking' of text to the concise use of headings, contents pages and indexes which are accurate, specific and focused on the learner's needs and goals.

The overall appearance of an instructional text plays a critical part in its impact, acceptability and ease of use. Learners' subjective assessments of the complexity of the content of information; their willingness to attempt particular tasks; and their impression of the value of the information is all influenced by the way in which information is visually presented.

A number of factors determine how well instructional text will be received by learners:

Typography

- It is generally accepted that text printed in lower case with few initial capital letters is easier to read than capital letters only. This is also the case for titles and headings.

- For general readership, the ideal character size of text is between 9 and 12 point. Type size has more effect on legibility than any other single typographic feature.

- Italics, bold type, reversed type and underlining are all useful as means of emphasizing text, but none are as legible as roman type for large bodies of text.

- The optimum length of line ranges from between 20 to 70 characters, depending on context.

- Proportionally-spaced text is easier to read than non-proportionally-spaced text.

- For instructional text, the choice of typeface, text justification, hyphenation and the semantic qualities of type are less important than the layout of the page.

Page layout

- The ease of retrieval and comprehension of printed text is affected more by the use that is made of space on a page, rather than the type.

- A single-column layout is most appropriate for the presentation of technical materials containing a large number of tables and diagrams.

- The use of 'white space' which emphasize headings can aid scan reading and provide useful space for learners' notes.

Graphics

- *Tables:* The ability to understand and interpret tabulated information requires special reading skills. Appropriate design of information in tables can help readers who may only have a weak grasp of these skills. Specific design decisions have to be taken in a way that is both sensitive to the internal structure of the data being presented and to the needs of the readers who want to use the information. Eliminating redundancy can be a false economy: removing information from a table so that it requires less space may mean that users have more problems trying to extract information from the table. Rules between columns and rows help readers capture the content and meaning of the table.

- *Diagrams:* Effective diagrams are instruments for reasoning about quantitative information. They not only show the data, but induce the viewer to think about the substance and not the method. They can present many numbers in a small space, making large data sets coherent. They can also encourage the eye to compare different sets of data and reveal the data at several layers of detail, from a broad overview to the fine structure. Many diagrams, however, are culturally determined: learners with little or no experience of their use may well find them incomprehensible.

- *Visual cues:* Visual cues direct the attention of learners to specific points in a text. Recall is significantly greater when pictorial and textual cues are used together, but not when either type of cue is used alone.

10.2.4 Research into illustration

Illustrations can play a significant role in developing learning concepts, not only at the initial point of learning but also when they are introduced into text as a means of recalling content at a later date. They can perform many functions which range from the provision of technical information to complementing prose-based information and stimulating attention.

There is little doubt that pictures are essential for communicating in print with people who cannot read. The most important factors which affect the decision to use illustrations for literate readerships are educational objectives and student characteristics. In such cases, illustrations are likely to be most effective when the content of the text is strongly visual.

There are shortcomings with some of the published research which focuses on simple illustrations such as line drawings, but which are not necessarily representative of those found in instructional texts. Furthermore, the precise mechanisms by which illustrations aid learning have proved difficult to determine. A model for the analysis of illustrations such as that provided by Goldsmith (1984) can help to overcome such difficulties and ensure that, where pictures are used in an educational context, they will be used to their best effect. The following points are particularly important:

- Characteristics of an individual learner (for example: age, ability, educational level; experience, culture and background) affect the ways in which an illustration is perceived and understood.

- The perception of illustrations is also, in part, a learned ability. Although fundamental responses to depth in pictures is present at early stages in development, responses are more sophisticated among populations who are continually exposed to pictorial materials.

- Effective devices for attracting, holding and directing attention, include colour, tonal contrast, position, size, and the isolation of objects.

- The arrangement of pictures with text is likely to have an effect on perception and comprehension, but significance of the effects on learning have proved difficult to measure.

- Problems arise in the presentation of arbitrary symbols and the application of colours when attempts are made to convey extended or figurative meanings. Not only do images and colours symbolize different things to people from different cultures, but the connotations of certain types of dress or environment may not be the same for artist and viewer. The acceptability of a depicted event is also an important consideration.

- Many authors note that engineering drawing, as a visual language, is essential for communicating technical information throughout the design and implementation phases of infrastructure development. Some believe that engineering drawing is a universal language. Others, however, recognize that the level of spatial ability necessary to visualize a three-dimensional object drawn on a plane surface varies between groups of students, and that the differences are even greater between cultures where alternative visual codes are employed for defining pictorial space.

- The emphasis on developing visualization skills for the development professional lies in the interpretation of drawings, rather than on their production.

- Little use is made in engineering drawing of many pictorial depth cues which help most people associate pictures with the physical world, and there appears to be little research concerning the relative merits of different types of two-dimensional projections of three-dimensional space. The need for such research takes on a greater significance when technical illustrations are required to 'stand alone', i.e: without verbal explanations by a tutor.

10.3. Conclusions drawn from the research results and analysis

Part II of the research presented questions which arose from the literature reviewed in Part I. The research hypotheses were formulated and tested as a means of addressing these questions. The results were presented, and analysed and discussed in Chapters 8 and 9 respectively. This section presents the conclusions.

10.3.1 Hypothesis H1

The first hypothesis (see Section 6.4) stated that isometric projections are easier to understand than third-angle projections. Analysis of the results demonstrated that this was certainly the case for the groups of subjects studied, and would most probably be the case for a wider population as defined by the list of variables presented in Section 6.3.

These results imply that an isometric projection is likely to be more effective in revealing the nature of an object or structure where there is a choice is to be made between representing the three-dimensional nature of the object or structure in either third-angle or isometric projection.

This does not invalidate the use of third-angle projections, however, which may be the most appropriate way of presenting design details. It appears, nonetheless, that the difference in understanding between the two types of projection are so significant that representing an object or structure in a learning context with a third-angle projection alone could limit the opportunity for learning.

10.3.2 Hypothesis H2

The second hypothesis stated that the ability of adult learners to understand the pictorial conventions of isometric and third-angle projection is significantly affected by one or more of the variables listed in Section 6.3.

Whilst the conclusions from the analysis of the results of H1 reported above were clear to draw, the conclusions to be drawn from the results of the tests relating to H2 are not. The results reject the hypothesis, except in certain instances. Of the variables listed, it appears that *English as first language*; *Ethnic origin*; and *Economic region* could influence the understanding of isometric projections, and that *Gender* could influence the understanding of third-angle projections. Except for *English as first language* in respect of isometric projections, however, these results are marginal. This leads to the general conclusion that, for the populations studied, illustrations prepared using either of these types of projection *per se*, would neither significantly advantage, nor disadvantage any particular group of adult learners. Other features of the illustrations, such as annotations, may well have an effect, but these have not formed part of this study.

10.3.3 Hypothesis 3

Test R4, which relates to the third hypothesis, was designed to assess whether recognition of the laws of linear perspective as a primary means of understanding pictorial space is significantly affected by one or more of the listed variables. This test, therefore, was concerned with the *preferred* methods of pictorial perception, and not with ability.

It was reported that the methodology for testing Hypothesis H3 was experimental, and that the reliability of the results is therefore questionable. Taking the results at face value, however, it appears that a number of variables could well influence the ways in which subjects interpret pictorial space as defined by the laws of linear perspective. *Age*, *Artistic background*, *Educational level*, *English as first language*, *Ethnic origin*, *Economic region*, and *Work experience* are all, potentially, influential variables.

10.4. Proposals for further study

It is clear from the discussion above that a number of conclusions can be drawn from both the literature review presented in Part I, and from the analyses of the research results presented in Part II. As such, the purpose, aims and objectives of the research have been fulfilled.

The focus of the research allowed for the detailed study of particular drawing systems. It follows that extended studies of these and other drawing systems, and how their use affects the comprehension of illustrations in instructional text, will lead to enhanced understanding.

An important subject for additional study at the technical/professional level, in particular, is the cross-cultural variations in the understanding of the laws of linear perspective. Additionally, a study of cross-cultural variations in the understanding of sectional elevations and 'cut-away' three-dimensional views would also enhance understanding, as too would an assessment of the impact of colour on the understanding of technical illustrations now that low-cost colour-printing is becoming more widely available.

References

Aslanian, Carol and Brickell, Henry M. (1980) *Americans in Transition: Life Changes as Reasons for Adult Learning,* College Entrance Examination Board, Princeton, New Jersey.

Ausubel, David P. (1968) *Educational Psychology: A Cognitive View,* Holt, Rinehart, and Winston, New York.

Bartrum, David (1982) 'The perception of semantic quality in type: differences between designers and non-designers', *Information Design Journal,* 3 (1), pp.38-50.

Beach, Richard J. (1987) 'Tabular typography', in J.C. van Vliet (ed.) *Text processing and document manipulation,* Cambridge University Press, London.

Beck, Charles R. (1984) 'Visual cueing strategies: pictorial, textual and combinational effects', *Educational Communication and Technology Journal,* 32 (4) pp.207-216.

Bernt, F.L. and Bugbee, A.C. (1993) 'Study practices and attitudes related to academic success in a distance learning programme', *Distance Education,* 14 (1), pp.97-112.

Bilham, T. and Gilmour, R. (1995) 'Distance Education in Engineering for Developing Countries', *Education Research Serial No. 13,* Overseas Development Administration, London.

Bradley, Sarah Murray (1995). *How People Use Pictures: An Annotated Bibliography and Review for Development Workers,* IIED, London.

Brandt, H. (1945) *The Psychology of Seeing,* Philosophical Library, New York.

Bratt, J. (1978) 'Pictorial Prescription Labels', *Educational Broadcasting International,* 11 (3), pp.143-148.

Brody, P. (1981) 'Research on pictures in instructional texts: the need for a broadened perspective', *Educational Communication and Technology Journal,* 29 (2) pp.93-100.

Brundage, D., Keane, R., and Mackneson, R. (1993) 'Application of learning theory to the instruction of adults', in Thelma Barer-Stein and James A. Draper (eds.) *The craft of teaching adults*, pp.131-144, Toronto, Ontario.

Brundage, D.H. and MacKeracher, D. (1980) *Adult Learning Principles and Their Application to Program Planning,* Ministry of Education, Toronto, Ontario.

Burge, E.J. and Howard, J.L. (1990) 'Audio-conferencing in graduate education: A Case Study', *The American Journal of Distance Education,* 4 (2), pp.3-13.

Burnhill, P., Hartley, J., and Young M. (1976) 'Tables in Text', *Applied Ergonomics,* 7 (1), pp.13-18.

Buswell, G.T. (1935) *How People Look at Pictures,* University of Chicago Press.

Campbell Keagan Ltd (1990) *Income Support: New brochure development,* Campbell Keagan Ltd for the Department of Social Security, London.

Carpenter, P.A. and Just, M.A. (1977) 'Reading comprehension as the eyes see it', in M.A. Just and P.A. Carpenter (eds) *Cognitive Processes in Comprehension,* Erlbaum, New Jersey.

Charrow, V. and Redish, J.C. (1980) *A study of standardised headings for warranties,* Technical Report 6, American Institutes for Research.

Child, Dennis (1981) *Psychology and the Teacher* (3rd ed.) Holt, Rinehart and Winston, London.

Cohen, Louis, and Holliday, Michael (1984) *Statistics for Social Scientists,* Harper and Row, London.

Coldeway, D.O., MacRury, K., and Spencer, R. (1980) *Distance education from the learner's perspective: The results of individual learner tracking at Athabasca University,* Edmonton, Alberta.

Concise Oxford Dictionary of Current English (6th ed.) (1976) Clarendon Press, Oxford.

Constable, H., Campbell, R., and Brown, R. (1988) 'Sectional drawings from science textbooks: an experimental investigation into pupils' understanding'. *British Journal of Educational Psychology*, 58 (1), pp.89-102.

Cook, B.L. (1980) 'Picture communication in Papua New Guinea', *Educational Broadcasting International*, 13 (2) pp.78-83.

Cripwell, Kenneth R. (1989) 'Non-picture visuals for communication in health learning manuals', *Health Education Research*, 4 (3), pp.297-304.

Davies, T.N. (1973) 'Visual perception of engineering drawings', *Engineering Designer*, 4, pp.22-31.

Davis, Larry N. and McCallon, Earl (1975) 'Planning, Conducting and Evaluating Workshops', in *Learning Concepts*, Austin, Texas.

Dawson, J. (1967a) 'Cultural and physiological influences upon spatial-perceptual processes in West Africa: Part I', *International Journal of Psychology*, 2 (2), pp.115-128.

Dawson, J. (1967b) 'Cultural and physiological influences upon spatial-perceptual processes in West Africa: Part II', *International Journal of Psychology*, 2 (3), pp.171-185.

Department of Typography and Graphic Communication, Reading University (1999) http://www.rdg.ac.uk/AcaDepts/lt

Deregowski, J.B. (1968) 'Pictorial recognition in subjects from a relatively pictureless environment', *African Social Research*, 5, pp.356-364.

Deregowski, J.B., Muldrow, E.S. and Muldrow, W.F. (1972) 'Pictorial recognition in a remote Ethiopian population', *Perception*, 1, pp.417-425.

DFID (1998) *Guidance Manual on Water Supply and Sanitation Programmes*, Department for International Development, London.

Duncan, H.F., Gourlay, H. and Hudson, W. (1973) *A Study of Pictorial Perception among Bantu and White Primary School Children in South Africa*, Witwaterstrand University Press, Johannesburg.

Dwyer, F.M. (1972) *A Guide for Improving Visualized Instruction,* Learning Services, State College, Pennsylvania.

Duchastel, P. (1980) 'Research on illustrations in text: issues and perspectives'. *Educational Communication and Technology Journal,* 28 (4) pp.283-287.

Egan, M.W., Sebastian, J., and Welch, M. (1991) 'Effective television teaching: Perceptions of those who count most: distance learners', *Proceedings of the Rural Education Symposium,* Nashville, Tennessee.

Elsheikh, Ahmed (1995) *Drawing for Civil Engineers,* McGraw-Hill, London.

Fales, Ann and Greey, Mary (1981) 'The Puzzle of Mid-Life Learning: What are the Pieces?', *Yearbook of Adult and Continuing Education,* Marquis Academic Media, Chicago.

FDS (1986) *Inland Revenue Publications Survey,* FDS Market Research Ltd, London.

Fisher, D. (1976) Spatial factors in reading and research: the case for space', in R.A. Monty and J.W. Senders (eds.) *Eye movements and Psychological Processes,* Erlbaum, New Jersey.

Franceys, R.W.A. (1996) *Education and Training Opportunities with WEDC,* unpublished, WEDC, Loughborough University, UK.

Frase, L.T. and Schwartz, B.J. (1979) 'Typographical cues that facilitate comprehension', *Journal of Educational Psychology* 71 (2).

Freire, Paulo (1974) *The Pedagogy of the Oppressed,* Seabury Press, New York.

Friedman, S.L and Stevenson, M.B. (1975) 'Developmental changes in the understanding of implied motion in two-dimensional pictures', *Child Development*, 46, pp.773-778.

Fuglesang, Andreas (1982) *About Understanding: Ideas and Observations on Cross-Cultural Communication,* Dag Hammarskjold Foundation, Upsalla.

Fussell, D. and Haaland, A. (1978) 'Communicating with pictures in Nepal: Results of practical study used in visual education', *Educational Broadcasting International,* 11 (1) pp.25-31.

Garland, K. (1982) 'The use of short-term feedback in the preparation of technical and instructional illustration', in *Research in Illustration: Conference Proceedings Part II,* pp.63-80, Brighton Polytechnic.

Ghent, L. (1956), 'Perception of overlapping and embedded figures by children of different ages', *American Journal of Psychology,* 69, pp.575-587.

Gibson, J.J. (1950) *The Perception of the Visual World,* Houghton-Mifflin, Boston, Massachusetts.

Goldsmith, Evelyn (1984) *Research into Illustration: an approach and a review,* Cambridge University Press, London.

Goody, J. (1977) *The domestication of the savage mind,* Cambridge University Press, London.

Greenberg, J. (1978) 'Blind drawings: a new perspective', *Science News,* 114 (20) pp.332-333.

Greenfield, Susan (1999) 'The Future Could Be Too Much Fun'. Transcript of the 1999 Richard Dimbleby Lecture, BBC, London. (http://www.bbc.co.uk/science/humanbody/dimbleby.shtml : 1 December, 1999)

Gregory, M. and Poulton, E.C. (1970) 'Even versus uneven right-hand margins and the rate of comprehension in reading', *Ergonomics,* 13 pp.427-434.

Haber, R. (1978) 'Visual perception', *Annual Review of Psychology,* 29, pp.31-59.

Hagen, M.A. and Glick, R. (1977) 'Pictorial perspective: perception of size, linear and texture perspective in children and adults', *Perception,* 6 (6), pp.675-684.

Hagen, M.A. and Jones, R.K. (1978) 'Cultural effects on pictorial perception', in H. Pick and R. Walk (eds.) *Perception and Experience,* pp.171-212, Plenum Press, New York.

Hartley, J. (1979) 'Space and structure in instructional text', in: R.S. Easterby and H.J.G. Zwaga, (eds.) *Information Design: The design and evaluation of signs and printed material,* John Wiley and Sons Ltd, Chichester, UK.

Hartley, J. (1980) 'Underlining can make a difference', *Journal of Educational Research,* 73 (4), pp.218-224.

Hartley, J. (1981) 'Eighty ways of improving instructional texts', IEEE Transactions on Professional Communication, 24 (1), pp.17-27.

Hartley, J. (1982) 'Information mapping: a critique', *Information Design Journal,* 3 (1), pp.51-58.

Hartley, J. (1994) *Designing Instructional Text* (3rd ed.) Kogan Page, London.

Hartley, J. (1998) *Learning and Studying: A Research Perspective,* Routledge, London.

Hartley, J. and Trueman, M. (1983) 'The effects of headings in text on recall, search and retrieval', *British Journal of Educational Psychology,* 53 (2) pp.205-214.

Hartley, J. and Trueman, M. (1985) 'A research strategy for text designers: the role of headings', *Instructional Science,* 14 (2), pp.99-157.

Hayes, C.J.A. and King, W.L. (1967) 'Two types of instruction for size and distance judgements of objects presented on a two-dimensional plane', *Perception and Psychophysics,* 2, pp.556-558.

Hergenhahn, B.R. (1988) *An Introduction to Theories of Learning* (3rd ed.) Prentice-Hall, New Jersey.

Holmes, A.C. (1963) *A Study of Understanding of Visual Symbols in Kenya,* The Overseas Visual Aid Centre, London.

Holt, J. (1982) *How Children Learn*, Penguin, London.

Hochberg, J. (1972) 'The representation of things and people', in E.H. Gombrich, J Hochberg and M. Black (eds.) *Art, Perception and Reality*, pp.47-94, Johns Hopkins University Press, Baltimore, Maryland.

Hudson, W. (1960) 'Pictorial Depth Perception in Sub-Cultural Groups in Africa', *The Journal of Social Psychology*, 52, pp.183-208.

Ince, M.E. (1997) Personal communication.

Jenkins, J. (1978) 'Using pictures in non-formal education' *Educational Broadcasting International*, 11 (1), pp.32-38.

Jude, D.V. and Matkin, R.B. (1983) *Civil Engineering Drawing* (2nd ed.), Granada, London.

Keenan, Stacey A. (1984) 'Effects of chunking and line length on reading efficiency', *Visible Language*, 18 (1), pp.61-80.

Kelly, K.L. (1965) 'Twenty-two colors of maximum contrast', *Color Engineering*, 3, pp.26-27.

Kempson, E. and Moore, N. (1994) *Designing Public Documents*, Policy Studies Institute, London.

Kennedy, J.M. (1974) *A Psychology of Picture Perception*, Jossey-Bass, San Francisco.

Kennedy, J.M. and Ross, A.S. (1975) 'Outline picture perception by the Songe of Papua', *Perception*, 4, pp. 391-406.

Kidd, J.R. (1973) *How Adults Learn*, Association Press, New York.

Kimble, G.A. (1961) *Hilgard and Marquis Conditioning and Learning* (2nd ed.), Prentice-Hall, New Jersey.

Knox, Alan B. (1977) *Adult Development and Learning*, Jossey-Bass, San Francisco.

Lefrere, Paul (1983) *Effective forms: A case study of the development and testing of two postal forms for Supplementary Benefit,* The Open University Press, Milton Keynes, UK.

Lewis, C. and Walker, P. (1989) 'Typographic influences on reading', British Journal of Psychology, 80 (2), pp.241-257.

Linney, Bob (1995) *Pictures, People and Power: People-Centred Visual Aids for Development,* Macmillan, London.

Lunzer, E.A. (1968) *The Regulation of Behaviour: Volume 1,* Staples, London.

Martin, E.E., and Rainey, L. (1993) 'Student achievement and attitude in a satellite-delivered high school science course', *The American Journal of Distance Education,* 7 (1), pp.54-61.

McCoy, Vivian Rogers (1980) *A Life Transition Reader,* Adult Life Resource Center, University of Kansas.

McCrosky, J.C. and Anderson, J.F. (1976) 'The Relationship Between Communication Apprehension and Academic Achievement Among College Students', *Human Communication Research,* 3, pp.73-81.

McKinley, John (1978) *Participants Manual for Participation Training Institute,* Consortium for Human Resources, Indianapolis.

Moore, M.G., Thompson, M.M., Quigley, A.B., Clark, G.C. and Goff, G.G. (1990) *The effects of distance learning: A summary of the literature,* Research Monograph No. 2, American Center for the Study of Distance Education, Pennsylvania State University.

Moriarty, S.E. and Scheiner, E.C. 'A study of close set text type', *Journal of Applied Psychology,* 69 (4) pp.700-702.

Morgan, A. (1991) *Research into student learning in distance education,* University of South Australia, Victoria, Australia.

Morris, C. (1938) *Foundations of the Theory of Signs,* Vols.1 and 2, University of Chicago Press, Chicago.

MIL Research Ltd (1986a) *Employers' Guide to PAYE: A report on a qualitative study into employers' response to a new style and format for the Guide,* MIL Research Ltd for the Inland Revenue and the Central Office of Information, London.

MIL Research Ltd (1986b) *Reform of social security client group targeting: report on a qualitative and quantitative research study,* MIL Research Ltd for the Central Office of Information and the Department of Health and Social Security, London.

Misanchuk, E.A. (1992) *Preparing Instructional Text: Document design using desktop publishing,* Educational Technology Publications, New Jersey.

Morgan, Peter (1990) *Rural Water Supplies and Sanitation,* Macmillan, London.

Mundy-Castle, A.C. (1966) 'Pictorial depth perception in Ghanaian children', *International Journal of Psychology,* 1 (4), pp.289-300.

Munn, N.L., Fernald, D.L. and Fernald, P.S. (1972) *Introduction to Psychology,* Houghton Mifflin, Boston.

Nova Research Ltd (1986) *Revised P35 tax form diagnostic research,* Nova Research Ltd for the Central Office of Information and the Inland Revenue, London.

Owoeye, E.M. and Smith, S.E. (1987), *Engineering Drawing,* Macmillan, London.

Poulton, E.C. (1959) 'Effects of printing types and formats on the comprehension of scientific journals', *Nature,* 184, pp.1824-1825.

Reed, R.A. (1997) Personal communication.

Reid, D.J. and Miller, G.J.A. (1980) 'Pupils' perception of biological pictures and its implications for readability studies of biology textbooks', *Journal of Biological Education,* 14 (1), pp.59-69.

Reynolds, Linda (1984) 'The legibility of printed scientific and technical information', in: R.S. Easterby and H.J.G. Zwaga, (eds.) *Information Design: The design and evaluation of signs and printed material,* John Wiley and Sons Ltd, Chichester, UK.

Rock, I. Shallo, J. and Schwartz, F. (1978) 'Pictorial depth and related constancy effects as a function of recognition', *Perception,* 7 (1), pp.3-19.

Ross, L.R., and Powell, R. (1990) 'Relationships between gender and success in distance education courses: A preliminary investigation', *Research in Distance Education,* 2 (2), pp.10-11.

Rowe, Camille L. (1982) 'The connotative dimensions of selected display typefaces', *Information Design Journal,* 3 (1), pp.30-37.

Rowntree, Derek (1990) *Teaching Through Self-Instruction: How to Develop Open Learning Materials,* (rev. ed.), Kogan Page, London.

Rowntree, Derek (1994) *Preparing Materials for Open, Distance and Flexible Learning: An Action Guide for Teachers and Trainers,* Kogan Page, London.

Rutherford, R.B., Casey, R.J., Hasterok, G.S. and Howell, K. (1979) 'Function of color in learning an assembly task by learning disabled adolescents', *Perceptual and Motor Skills,* 48 (3), pp.1195-1198.

Saiet, R.A. (1979) 'Children's understanding of implied motion cues', ERIC Document ED 172801.

Schlosser, C.A., and Anderson, M.L. (1994) *Distance education: A review of the literature,* Iowa Distance Education Alliance, Iowa State University.

Schuemer, R. (1993) *Some psychological aspects of distance education*, Institute for Research into Distance Education, Hagen, Germany.

Segall, M., Campbell, D. and Herskovitz, M. (1996) *The Influence of Culture on Visual Perception*, The Bobbs-Merrill Co. Inc., New York.

Shaw, B. (1969) *Visual Symbols Survey: Report on the Recognition of Drawings in Kenya*, Centre for Educational Development Overseas, London.

Shaw, Esther (2000) *Women Working Together: Course notes*, unpublished.

Sheehy, Gail (1976) *Passages: Predictable Crises of Adult Life*, E.P. Dutton, New York.

Siegel, S. (1956) *Non-parametric Statistics for the Behavioral Sciences*, McGraw Hill, Tokyo.

Smith, J. and Watkins, H. (1972) *An Investigation into Some Aspects of the Illustration of Primary School Books*, Typography Unit, University of Reading.

Smith, Robert M. (1983) *Learning How to Learn: Applied Theory for Adults*, The Open University Press, Milton Keynes, UK.

Smout, I.K. (1996) from the unpublished presentation: *25 Years of WEDC*, Burleigh Court, Loughborough University, UK.

Souder, W.E. (1993). 'The effectiveness of traditional vs. satellite delivery in three management of technology master's degree programs', *The American Journal of Distance Education*, 7 (1), pp.37-53.

Spencer, H. (1969) *The Visible Word*, Lund Humphries, London.

Spencer, H. and Shaw, A. (1971) 'Letter Spacing and Legibility', *British Printer*, 84, pp.84-86

Spencer, H., Reynolds, L. and Coe, B. (1973) *A Report on the Relative Legibility of Alternative Letter Shapes*, Readability of Print Research Unit, Royal College of Art, London.

Spencer, H., Reynolds, L. and Coe, B. (1977) *The Effects of Show-through on the Legibility of Printed Text,* Readability of Print Research Unit, Royal College of Art, London.

Spencer, J. (1965) 'Experiments on Engineering Drawing Comprehension', *Ergonomics,* 8, pp.93-109.

Stark, Heather A. (1988) 'What do paragraph markings do?', *Discourse Processes,* 11 (3), pp.275-303.

Stubbs, M. (1980) Language and Literacy: The sociolinguistics of reading and writing, Routledge and Kegan Paul Ltd, London.

Suen, C.Y. and Komoda, M.K. (1986) 'Legibility of digital type-fonts and comprehension in reading', in J.C. van Vliet (ed.) *Text processing and document manipulation,* Cambridge University Press, London.

Swarts, H., Flower, L.S. and Hayes, J.R. (1980) *How headings in documents can mislead readers*, Technical Report 9, American Institutes for Research.

Tennyson, R.D. (1978) 'Pictorial support and specific instructions and design variables for children's concept and rule learning', *Educational Communication and Technology Journal,* 26 (4) pp.291-300.

Threlkeld, R., and Brzoska, K. (1994) 'Research in distance education', in B. Willis (ed.), *Distance Education: Strategies and Tools,* Educational Technology Publications Inc., New Jersey.

Tinker, M.A. (1963) *Legibility of Print,* Iowa State University Press, Iowa.

Travers, R.M.W. (1969) 'A study of the advantages and disadvantages of using simplified visual presentations in instructional materials' *ERIC Document ED 031951.*

Tufte, Edward R. (1983) *The Visual Display of Quantitative Information,* Graphics Press, Cheshire, Connecticut.

Vanderplas, J.M. and Vanderplas, J.H. (1980) 'Some factors affecting legibility of printed materials for older adults', *Perceptual and Motor Skills,* 50 (3), pp.923-932.

Verduin, J.R. and Clark, T.A. (1991*) Distance education: The foundations of effective practice.* Jossey-Bass, San Francisco.

WEDC (2000) *Education and Training Opportunities with WEDC: 2000-2001,* WEDC, Loughborough University, UK.

Whalley, P.C. and Fleming, R.W. (1975) 'An experiment with a simple recorder of reading behaviour' *Programmed Learning and Educational Technology,* 12, pp.120-124.

Wheildon, C. (1984) *Communicating, or just making pretty shapes: a study of the validity — or otherwise — of some elements of typographic design,* Newspaper Advertising Bureau of Australia.

Whittington, N. (1987) 'Is instructional television educationally effective? A research review', *The American Journal of Distance Education,* 1 (1), pp.47-57.

Wilkes, C.W., and Burnham, B.R. (1991) 'Adult learner motivations and electronics distance education', *The American Journal of Distance Education,* 5 (1), pp.43-50.

Willis, B. (1993) *Distance education: A practical guide,* Educational Technology Publications, Englewood Cliffs, New Jersey.

Willis, B. (1995) *Distance Learning at a Glance,* Engineering Outreach, College of Engineering, University of Idaho. (http://www.uidaho.edu/evo/distglan.html)

World Bank (2000) *The Global Distance Learning Network,* World Bank, Washington DC.

Wright, P. (1979) *Communicating with the Public,* Central Office of Information, London.

Wright, P. (1981) 'Tables in text: The subskills needed for reading formatted information', in L.J. Chapman (ed.) *The reader and the text,* Proceedings of the 17th UKRA Conference, Warwick, Heineman, London.

Wright, P. (1982). 'The Design of Tables and Flowcharts', in D.H. Jonassen. *The Technology of Text,* pp. 317-340. Educational Technology Publications, New Jersey.

Young, Michael, Perraton, Hilary, Jenkins, Janet, and Dodds, Tony (1991) *Distance Teaching for the Third World: The Lion and the Clockwork Mouse* (2nd ed.), International Extension College, Cambridge.

Zaki, W.M. (1975) *Education of the People,* People's Open University, Islamabad.

Appendices

Subject Profile Form

Please complete both sides of this form using BLOCK CAPITALS. You may complete it anonymously if you wish by leaving the boxes marked * blank

Surname or family name *	Office use

Forename/s or other name/s *

Title (e.g. Mr, Mrs, Ms, Dr, Prof etc.) *	**Gender** (please circle) Male / Female	**Nationality**
Country of birth	**Main country of childhood**	**Country of permanent residence**

Age (please circle)

Under 20	21-30	31-40	41-50	51-60	61 or over

Current address *

Town/City *

County / State / Region *

Country

Telephone *	**Fax** *	**Email** *

Highest educational level attained (if any)

Status or profession (e.g. student, water engineer, etc.)

Number of years work experience (please circle)

Under 5	5-10	11-15	21-25	26-30	31 or over

Native language/s

Fluency in other languages (please indicate level/s of fluency – e.g. spoken, spoken & written, or give qualification)

If English is not your first language, what is your highest English language qualification (if any)

I describe my ethnic origin as (e.g. Chinese, Black African, Middle-Eastern, Asian, White European,)

I describe my religious background as (e.g. Moslem, Hindu, Jewish, Christian)

Number of years formal training and/or experience in engineering drawing/technical illustration (please circle)

None   0-3   4-6   7-9   Over 10   Level attained: _____

Artistic background (please give details of any special artistic interests or achievements, if any)

_____

_____

My vision is (please circle and give details of any sight impairment e.g. colour blindness)

Good-Excellent   Adequate   Poor

Details

_____

I am left-handed/right-handed/ambidextrous*   **I am/am not dyslexic***

(*Please delete as appropriate)

Brief description of educational background including country

Up to age 11   _____

Age 11-18   _____

Age 18 or over   _____

Current course of study (if applicable)   _____

I would/would not* be willing to participate in further tests of this nature at a later date. (* *Please delete as appropriate*)

Thank you for your co-operation.

Rod Shaw
Water, Engineering and Development Centre (WEDC)
Loughborough University
Leicestershire LE11 3TU UK

Tasks R1-4: Instructions

Task R1: Isometric projection (8 minutes)

Please refer to Sheet R1

Contained within each of the boxes (1-10) is an incomplete isometric drawing of a single solid object.

Complete each drawing by adding two solid straight lines. Note that a solid line represents the visible meeting of two planes.

Task R2: Visualisation of plans from isometric projections (8 minutes)

Please refer to Sheet R2

Contained within each of the boxes (1-10) is an isometric drawing of a single solid object.

By referring to each set of drawings one at a time, draw on the paper provided a linear representation of each object as though seen directly from above.

Task R3: Third-angle projection (8 minutes)

Please refer to Sheet R3

Contained within each of the boxes (1-10) is a set of linear projections of three different views of a single solid object. There are views as seen from above (a), from the front (b) and from the right side (c). An example is given. One or more of the projections from each set is incomplete.

Complete the set of projections by adding two solid straight lines. These lines may be adjacent or apart. Note that a solid line represents the visible meeting of two planes. A dashed line represents the 'hidden' meeting of two planes.

Task R4: False perspective (10 minutes)

Please refer to Sheet R4

Pictured on this sheet is a copy of an engraving by William Hogarth, an eighteenth century English artist. Hogarth deliberately constructed this picture to illustrate ambiguities in the representation of pictorial space when the rules of perspective are broken. The picture contains 'impossible' occurrences when viewed according to the laws of perspective.

Using the pen provided, locate and describe any area of the picture where you perceive an 'impossible' occurrence to be taking place. An example is given.